Mental Health

and

High Sensitivity

Manuela Pérez Chacón

Antonio Chacón

Juan Moisés de la Serna

Editorial Tektime

2021

"Mental Health and High Sensitivity"

Written by Manuela Pérez Chacón, Antonio Chacón and Juan Moisés de la Serna

1st Edition: december 2021

© Juan Moisés de la Serna, 2021

© Ediciones Tektime, 2021

All rights reserved

Distributed by Tektime

https://www. traduzionelibri.it

About the authors:

Manuela Pérez Chacón

Degree in Psychology, Ph.D. student in the inter-university program on Psychology of Human Resources at the University of Seville and the University of Valencia. Specialist in Clinical Psychology. Specialist in Industrial Psychology. University Specialist in Special Education: Therapeutic Pedagogy. Professional Expert in "Psychological disorders in children and adolescents." Master in Occupational Risk Prevention, specializing in Safety, Hygiene, Ergonomics, and Psychosociology.

Master of Psychology with over 10 years of experience in the areas of health and psychosocial risk prevention. Specialized in clinical therapy and occupational psychology. Expert in Children and Adolescent Mental Disorders. Member-founder of the Child-Youth Mental Health Unit of the Hospital Jerez Puerta del Sur (USMIJ-Clínica Jerez). Gold Medal to Professional Merit by the General Council of Industrial Relations and Labor Sciences, PREVER 2018 Awards, for her research in the field of Psychosocial Risks in the Workplace. Member of the Official College of Psychologists of Western Andalusia number AN-06014.

President of the Spanish Association of High Sensitivity Professionals (HSP Spain). Psychologist

Specializing in HSP (Highly Sensitive Persons) and referring physician in Spain as an expert in High Sensitivity. Public speaker specializing in Child Psychology and Sensory Processing Sensitivity (SPS) in Children. First Spanish woman certified as a psychologist specializing in High Sensitivity (Acknowledged Professional by Elaine Aron). Has been interviewed several times in well-known media channels such as Cadena SER, La1 de RTVE, or El Pais.

Antonio Chacón

Expert in psychosocial risk management with 15 years of experience in External Prevention Services (EPS). Ph.D. Student in the Psychology of Human Resources program at the University of Seville. Assistant professor at the International University of La Rioja of the Masters in Occupational Risk Prevention and Masters in Systems Integration. (International University of La Rioja – UNIR).

Founder of the Association of Psychologists and High Sensitivity Professionals (HSP Spain). Awarded a Cruz de Honor (Cross of Honor) for health and Safety in the Workplace and awarded a Gold Medal of Professional Prestige by Forum Europe. Disseminator on the subject of High Sensitivity Trait in Organizations.

Juan Moisés de la Serna

Ph.D. of Psychology and Master in Neuroscience and Behavioral Biology, University Professor. To date, his research focuses on the potential factors influencing COVID -19 and on the short and long-term psychological and neurological complications after SARS CoV-2 infection in humans.

The most-read author in Spain in 2020 according to researchgate.net.

Scientific disseminator with more than 30 books published on Psychology and Neuroscience, including topics such as ADD, PDD, ASD, ADHD, EQ, MSD, High Capacity.

Prologue

The interest generated by our first book on High Sensitivity encouraged us to continue disseminating insight on this personality trait. This second book focuses more on the difficulties experienced by highly sensitive people as well as on the psychological abilities they possess. Knowing how to manage the trait of High Sensitivity is fundamental to achieving a maximum potential in the personal growth of the Highly Sensitive Person (HSP). Hence the importance of knowing how to meet the needs of highly sensitive children (HSC) from an early age. HSC children become HSP adults. Solve the issue in childhood and you avoid the need for treatments later on.

Throughout life, the HSP can go through transient psychological problems or disorders derived from mismanagement of their trait. In these pages, we share real examples of people who have come to a psychology consultation looking for a solution to their "bumps in the road". Many HSPs discover it in the wake of one of these ups and downs in their lives. Knowing how to take the right path, choosing to have people close to them who respect the HSP trait, and learning to set limits, are the objectives most demanded by the HSPs who are treated by a mental health professional.

This book aims to help both the reader, as well as the health or medical professional. Based on our experience as professional experts of High Sensitivity we are offering solutions to the problems that arise from being an HSP, sharing examples of people who have gone through the same stages, as well as showing some of the most common disorders derived from having this particular personality trait. Although being an HSP or HSC is not a disorder, it is necessary to learn to adapt to today's society until society becomes better acquainted with High Sensitivity.

Manuela Pérez
www.HSPespana.org

Index

Chapter 1. Introduction to the study of the relationship between High Sensitivity and Mental Health

Whether you are a highly sensitive person or a mental health professional, you will benefit from reading this book. You may be a person who has discovered your highly sensitive trait as a result of not feeling too good about yourself. Or maybe you have spent years going to psychologists and psychiatrists, or have been looking for information until someone enlightened you with knowledge of the existence of Highly Sensitive People (HSP). You may be a professional who has cared for people you could not quite manage to understand, people who did not exactly have a disorder but there was something that prevented them from growing and continuing their journey in life with ease. Perhaps, your case is that of an individual who is having a hard time communicating with your partner because it seems that you are each speaking a different language since each one feels and perceives the world differently. You may have even left a job due to feeling like you did not fit in, whether with others or with repetitive and routine tasks.

We all indeed have sensitivity and it is also true that anyone may need at some point in their life to go to a psychology professional to resolve something whether small or big. This book aims to provide a way to work with highly sensitive people.

What is written here will help you not only to identify the trait but also to detect the psychological consequences of it from a psychology professional point of view. It addresses High Sensitivity (HS) or Sensory Processing Sensitivity (SPS) as seen by mental health experts, a contribution of experiences, studies, and scientific basis.

We will define what it means to be a highly sensitive person and your relationship with your environment from the strictest sense of the word. By reading this book you will learn about the most common psychological disorders and why highly sensitive people can suffer from them. You will understand the talent and the high capacity that highly sensitive people possess. All this is explained from a psychological point of view.

No doubt, the experiences of highly sensitive people serve as an example to us. However, we want to raise awareness among the HSP and HSC population of the importance of putting themselves in the hands of health professionals. It is the psychologists, counselors, pediatricians, and psychiatrists trained in High Sensitivity who are the most adept at solving the problems you may encounter.

It is essential to keep in mind that being highly sensitive is not the same as having a disorder. There are specific treatments currently being developed by scientific researchers. Possessing the trait of high sensitivity can lead you to suffer certain difficulties but also benefit from many advantages. The detection and diagnosis of any disorder associated with the trait should be left in the hands of mental health experts.

It is just as important to know who to turn to so you can find solutions if you possess the Highly Sensitive trait and questions arise, as well as to know that anyone around you can be an HSP.

It is also essential to trust the sciences, and psychology is one of them. Psychological techniques and treatments are a result of experiments and research that have been carried out by numerous experts over the years. In this book, we aim to make a connection between this scientific precision and the personality trait that we now colloquially know as High Sensitivity. The scientific name for this trait corresponds to Sensory Processing Sensitivity.

The Highly Sensitive Person has a way of perceiving and feeling that starts from birth and which is molded through experiences. It is a type of personality that includes a high capacity to process information about your surroundings. It makes you more aware of everything that enters through the five senses, especially in new or unexpected situations. The Theory of Positive Disintegration, known to many as a theory of "emotional development" by the Polish psychologist and psychiatrist Dabrowski during the beginning of psychology as a science, classified this ability as part of the different levels of human development.

This book will provide you with both information and possible solutions if you are someone who is involved in caring for the emotional needs of a person, whether that person is your child, your student, or your patient. In this book, you will find key information not found in other books since it explains the relationship between High Sensitivity and its possible consequences on an individual throughout their life. In addition to delivering a practical approach that can help highly sensitive people to manage their trait or help a person learn how to interact with highly sensitive children, the book provides data and sample consultations, as well as the most recent research on High Sensitivity.

This book is the result of a collaboration between high-sensitivity professionals and has been written in the form of a research project. It provides information collected from group therapies and individual psychology sessions conducted over several years in mental health departments and addresses some central issues of the daily work of High Sensitivity professionals with children and adolescents. Care of children is a field of great concern regarding study and treatment, especially in the interest of the prevention of possible mental disorders. Young people are the human potential of the near future in companies.

We have focused on the symptoms that derive from the presence of the highly sensitive trait in an individual under the perspective of the diagnostic axes of the Diagnostic and Statistical Manual of Mental Disorders (DSM—5). Risk factors, current treatments, and prevention have been based on cognitive-behavioral therapies. The diagnosis and evaluation provide a comparison and bring to light the possible confusion with some disorders that have similar pathological signs. Regarding the research models described, they include scientific theories at an international level that have been instrumental in the discovery of the High Sensitivity trait.

At present, there is a lot of research that supports the existence of this peculiar trait in a portion of the world's population. Several scientists from different countries have provided contrasting data on this particular way of feeling, thinking, and acting.

Up until now, science has shown us through studies conducted, that approximately 20% of the population has High Sensitivity (Aron and Aron, 1997). These are people with an innate ability to observe the smallest details and they do so unconsciously. They also need more rest time as they are easily overstimulated and must learn to manage their emotions in the face of excessive noise or crowded places. They show strong emotional responses and sometimes require more downtime. Likewise, the authors affirm that of this percentage of people who possess the trait of high sensitivity, 70% are introverts.

The development of the Highly Sensitive Child scale and identification of sensitivity groups (Pluess, 2017), published in Developmental Psychology is also a statistical study. Among its results is the existence of three different groups with different levels of environmental sensitivity. It indicates that all living beings must be sensitive to their surroundings and classifies 25-35% as highly sensitive, 41-47% as intermediate, and 20-35% as low.

The Highly Sensitive Person presents characteristics from birth that accompany them throughout their lives. These characteristics affect their well-being and as a result, their mental health. Elaine Aron, a pioneer research psychologist in the United States, highlighted the following particularities of HSP people: they can unconsciously show a heightened awareness of and strong reaction when encountering stimuli in their surroundings, even when these are subtle. This intense emotional reaction is because everything, both positive and negative, affects the HSP more. They also experience high levels of arousal due to sensory stimulation to noises, smells, and other sensations. A high capacity for empathy and increased sensory sensitivity to stimuli, which is manifested by a heightened ability to differentiate sensations is also found in the HSP.

The highly sensitive person and highly sensitive children are individuals who come by these personality traits naturally. They could focus these traits toward a positive outcome avoiding a negative path provided they have an awareness of their uniqueness and the proper tools to cope with the difficulties that may arise along the way, as well as knowledge of how to enhance their strengths. They are people with a gift because of their great creativity and their ability to process information. But they are also people who can easily become stressed or who tend to avoid certain social situations. Hence, the importance of knowing whether or not you are a Highly Sensitive Person and whether or not your child is a

Highly Sensitive Child.

The highly sensitive person can be identified by the high levels of sensitivity he or she exhibits. These are people who are easily excited by the stimuli around them. Other characteristics to take into account are empathy and the ability to grasp information from their surroundings.

Those who possess the trait of high sensitivity, process information in a peculiar way. They analyze everything more thoroughly. They can understand how the other person feels and take the emotions they perceive to the extreme. Therefore, when day-to-day emotions are positive (joy, calmness, optimism, etc.), the HSP can control what he or she feels to his or her benefit. In this case, it is an advantage to be a highly sensitive person. Although, since it is a genetic trait, it's not something you can choose to be. You are simply born or not born with the trait of high sensitivity.

On the other hand, when the person is faced with a complex routine full of negative emotions (anger, sadness, anguish, etc.), psychological problems may appear. It is common to encounter difficult situations throughout life. That's what living is all about, having all kinds of experiences and learning how to deal with them. However, for the highly sensitive person, it is often difficult to make decisions because of emotional factors that are difficult to control.

The most common difficulties that arise after mismanagement of high sensitivity are low self-esteem, anxiety, stress, phobias, depression, and even borderline personality disorder. Some of the symptoms that indicate the need to seek professional help are insomnia, muscular pain, low mood, emotional tension, anger, etc. In children, symptoms such as insecurity, shyness, attention deficit, and irritability stand out.

This is not to say that highly sensitive people are more likely to experience psychological symptoms just because they were born with the trait of high sensitivity. We want to say that perhaps having greater sensitivity to stimuli may increase the activation of the person in general. That is, if a highly sensitive person has many experiences that generate extreme or negative emotions, he or she is exposing him or herself to more pressure. Their body is stressed by situations that may go unnoticed by people who are not highly sensitive. It is also possible that the sum of stressful experiences may cause physical symptoms in the highly sensitive person that would not even affect anyone else.

The brain of the highly sensitive person pays more attention to sensations in his body that could be considered insignificant whereas other people do not perceive these sensations. It remains to be seen whether highly sensitive people go to the doctor more because of problems or complaints that cannot be diagnosed as a specific disease.

One thing we do know is that highly sensitive people become more saturated with less stimulation than other people. Their sensory threshold is lower. That is, they are more affected by stimuli and therefore are more easily overexcited or overstimulated. No one works well under pressure or under the effects of overstimulation nor do we all perform equally well at work or school when faced with tasks that involve too much emotional stress.

It is, therefore, imperative for the highly sensitive person to learn to manage this intense influx of information when it causes problems in their routine. This will allow them to carry out daily tasks with peace of mind and naturalness. The solution should not be to refuse activities, but rather to get to know oneself well and develop psychological strategies. Social skills can also be learned or encouraged. It's is especially important to do a self-assessment in line with one's own emotions.

The emotional reaction of a highly sensitive person is more extreme or notable than that of any other person, even in the same situation. For example, two brothers of similar age are watching a dramatic movie, one of them cries desperately and the other does not. These situations need not be traumatic for the highly sensitive person, as long as they have learned to identify with their trait and accept what they cannot change about themselves.

A fairly common repercussion for highly sensitive people who have not identified their trait is to try to change the way they are. Fighting against one's nature is impossible and inadvisable. The perfectionism and self-criticism developed by the highly sensitive person must be aimed towards self-benefit. The key to healthy self-esteem for highly sensitive people lies in preventing these two traits from becoming disadvantages or psychological problems.

Therefore, good management of high sensitivity consists of taking advantage of such sensitivity thus avoiding the usual inconveniences that arise so that they do not lead to psychological problems such as anxiety, depression, or stress.

In short, highly sensitive people perceive stimuli more intensely, generating greater vividness in their emotions. The emotions that any person generates in their daily life can be positive or negative. The positive ones are, for example, joy, happiness, or enthusiasm. Whereas the negative ones can be sadness, apathy, or anguish. The highly sensitive person is more sensitive to stimuli. This means greater activation in general and, therefore, greater pressure and discomfort in the face of negative emotions. Increased emotional stress, coupled with not knowing how to manage one's emotions, can lead to psychological symptoms and even the onset of health problems. Therefore, people who identify with the trait of high sensitivity must learn to manage their emotions. Achieving this can sometimes be a challenge, or it can simply come naturally. By managing this skill, psychological problems, such as anxiety or stress, can be avoided.

References

Aron, A., Ketay, S., Hedden, T., Aron, E. N., Rose Markus, H. and Gabrieli, J. D. (2010). Temperament Trait of Sensory Processing Sensitivity Moderates Cultural Differences in Neural Response. Social Cognitive and Affective Neuroscience, 5(2-3), 219-226.

Aron, E. N.andAron, A. (1997). Sensory-processing Sensitivity and its Relation to Introversion and Emotionality. Journal of Personality and Social Psychology, 73(2), 345–368.

Aron, E. N., Aron, A. and Jagiellowicz, J. (2012). Sensory Processing Sensitivity: A Review in the Light of the Evolution of Biological Responsivity. Personality and Social Psychology Review, 16(3), 262–282.

Dabrowski, K. (1964). Positive Disintegration. Little Brown.

Dabrowski, K. (1967). Personality Shaping Through Positive Disintegration. Little Brown.

Dabrowski, K. (1972). Psychoneurosis Is Not An Illness. Gryf Publications.

Dabrowski, K., Kawczak, A. and Piechowski, M. M. (1970). Mental Growth: Through Positive Disintegration. Gryf Publications.

Dabrowski, K.andPiechowski, M. M. (1977). Theory of Levels of Emotional Development. Volumes I and II.

Dabor Science Publications.

Díaz-García, M. I. and Díaz-Sibaja, M. A. (2005). Daily Problems in Childhood Behavior. M.I. Comeche and M.A. Vallejo (Coor.), Therapy Manual of Childhood Behavior. Dykinson.

Pluess, M. (2017). Vantage Sensitivity: Environmental Sensitivity to Positive Experiences as a Function of Genetic Differences. Journal of Personality, 85(1), 38-50 - https//doi.org/10.1111/jopy.12218

Chapter 2. Characteristics of the Highly Sensitive Person

The highly sensitive person perceives the stimuli they receive from the environment around them focusing on the details. It is a process that is carried out unconsciously, almost without realizing it. All the information that a person receives through the senses, in new situations, is carefully analyzed. Sight, hearing, taste, touch, and smell are at the same level of development as in a non-HSP person, however, the perception received through these organs is more enhanced in the HSP.

Perceiving sensations as an HSP is similar to feeling both ends of a stimulus. They are affected by a very loud noise or will notice one that is very quiet. They enjoy intense flavors or will detect a mild ingredient added to a recipe. What each person is most sensitive to will vary from one HSP to another. Some show their sensitivity to tastes, others to sounds, light, smells, or textures. But they all have extreme and obvious sensitivity.

The difference between HSP and non-HSP people lies in the tastes or interests they present. Non-HSP people differ from HSP people in that they choose their interests or tastes, whether they prefer a type of food or a type of music. On the other hand, the HSP possesses a need that is superior to interest or taste, it is something innate that is not determined by the simple fact of taste itself. We could say that there is a biological force that drives the HSP to perceive and be able to feel both sides of the coin, so to speak. Many of the complaints are about feeling too hot or too cold. There seems to be no middle ground. Sometimes they require being surrounded by a lot of people and sometimes they require solitude. This incongruence in various situations generates a certain discord with the people with whom they live.

On the positive side, a highly sensitive person enjoys the details of life. They show it through the sensation that various particularities produce in them, such as a deep conversation, watching a sunrise, or visiting a museum. In personal relationships, love and friendship take on a higher meaning. At the same time, they enjoy the privacy they get in those moments when they are alone, where they can give free rein to their creativity. Many of them are good at drawing, dancing, or cooking, others have the intelligence to make good decisions or to help others. There are many different aspects in which the highly sensitive person stands out thanks to their creativity and emotionality.

Regarding the notion of time, the HSP requires time

alone to disconnect from their routine. Especially after experiencing times of high stimulation, their body asks for a space of relaxation, silence, and tranquility.

The emotions of a highly sensitive person are characterized by their flexibility to be triggered by stimulating situations. The existence of experiences that generate extreme emotions is a determining factor for the HSP. They are capable of enjoying the good to a fuller extent, but also of suffering much when experiencing that which hurts.

The nervous system of the HSP, acting in a predetermined way, reacts when stimulated by the emotions generated by what happens in their surroundings. The limbic system is the part of the brain responsible for producing emotions, generating neurochemical and hormonal responses. In this way, the emotion is associated with the experience. Emotion is an unconscious, basic, primitive impulse. However, when emotions associated with similar experiences are repeated, the person begins to give it a concrete value by forming a feeling towards it. The HSP externalizes these feelings through a fine and subtle sensitivity.

In addition to feeling deeply, the highly sensitive person thinks and acts as a reflective whole. Without noticing that they do so, they process information by reflecting before acting through detailed observation of stimuli. In the same way, they can pick up on hidden messages from other people, to notice signals that are transmitted without the need to say anything, thanks to their empathy. Dr. Bianca Acevedo (2014) has studied the part of the brain responsible for stimulating mirror neurons, which are responsible for the existence of empathy. A higher incidence of this type of neuron has been found in highly sensitive people. In this sense, the HSP has that innate ability to be able to put themselves in other people's shoes and know what the other person is feeling. On the other hand, having such capacity does not necessarily imply having the intention to act on it.

IRENA 5 YEARS OLD

When Irena's mother decided to go to the psychologist's office, she had been putting up with comments at family meals and gatherings with friends for years. With the best intentions, grandparents, aunts, uncles, sisters-in-law, and friends showed their interest in Irena's psychological health. Instead of thinking that there was nothing wrong with her, it was rather they who were neglecting recognizing diversity in personality. The phrases were repeated every weekend: "What does her pediatrician say?" "At her age, she should be eating everything, as my children do." "Does she have friends at school? She seems so quiet." "Has she been tested to see if she is gifted, hyperactive, or is there something wrong with her? She doesn't look happy." "Does she have to cry about everything?" "When she grows up, who will defend her?" "Does she always have to refuse everything? All the children are playing except her."

Irena's mother was very uncomfortable with such comments. At the same time, she knew that her daughter possessed at least average intelligence. She was also an affectionate, cheerful, happy, and sensitive child. Her mother had observed similar behavior in some of the girls at her school, which gave her peace of mind. That's why she was slow to go to a psychologist's office, to avoid having her daughter labeled because her intuition told her that Irena simply felt and behaved differently from her cousins and her friends' children. When she finally sought professional help, it was confirmed that there was no disorder. After some time, she found on the web, by chance, that there were HSC, highly sensitive children, thus unmasking the mystery of why Irena acted and sensed life in her own way.

JANE 38 YEARS OLD

Jane had spent her whole life trying to please the people around her, even if it meant discomfort for herself despite her growing awareness that she was losing more and more self-esteem because of her attitude. As a child, she was obedient, unable to say what she thought so as not to hurt her parents' feelings. As a teenager, she didn't have her own criteria. She let herself be "crushed", as she said, especially by her mother, who constantly manipulated her to mold her into the daughter she had designed. Her youth was filled with social problems with friends as she could not make her own decisions, she had not learned to do so. This also led to relationship problems, Jane was so empathetic that she gave everything without asking for anything in return, letting her fear of failure get the better of her.

The most traumatic experience Jane recounted was living with a partner who acted as if the world revolved around him and who had an exaggerated sense of his importance and entitlement. In therapy she discovered that her partner was narcissistic, a person who had to be the center of attention at all times and who needed continuous praise. A person whom she needed to praise constantly to have his approval and who would punish her if she didn't comply with his wishes.

Like most people, Jane thought she was different and that this was her lot in life. Two factors overlapped, being a highly empathetic person and her old-fashioned upbringing, that is, growing up hearing phrases such as: "Turn the other cheek." Or, "You're much prettier when you're quiet." Or, "Don't do to others what you don't want them to do to you."

In treatment, the starting point was Jane's recognition of the four highly sensitive person's trait factors. Secondly, they worked on social skills, especially assertiveness, and also improved her self-esteem. The patient learned to detect people who did not make her feel good and to defend herself against them. The fact that she had hit rock bottom in her relationship was also her salvation, as she sought professional help and realized that she should not allow another person to manipulate her, that she should not expect a narcissist to respect her sensitivity, nor should she have to continually praise him to get the slightest thing from him. Jane shook off her fear of failure, feeling proud to be herself and to be able to choose who she wants to share something with and what decisions to make. Now she is not afraid. She is not even afraid to make mistakes, as she prefers to make her own mistakes and learn from them rather than to not be herself.

References

Acevedo, B.P. (2016). The Highly Sensitive Brain: The Neural Correlates of Sensory Processing Sensitivity. Journal of the American Academy of Child and Adolescent Psychiatry, 55.

Acevedo, B. P., Aron, E. N., Aron, A., Sangster, M. D., Collins, N. and Brown, L. L. (2014). The Highly Sensitive Brain: An fMRI Study of Sensory Processing Sensitivity and Response to Others' Emotions. Brain and Behavior, 4(4), 580–594. https://doi.org/10.1002/brb3.242

Acevedo, B.P., Aron, E., Pospos, S. and Jessen, D. (2018). The Functional Highly Sensitive Brain: A Review of the Brain Circuits Underlying Sensory Processing Sensitivity and Seemingly Related Disorders. Philosophical Transactions of the Royal Society B: Biological Sciences, 373.

Acevedo, B.P., Santander, T., Marhenke, R., Aron, A.,and Aron, E. (2021). Sensory Processing Sensitivity Predicts Individual Differences in Resting-State Functional Connectivity Associated with Depth of Processing. Neuropsychobiology 80, 185 - 200.

Brown, L., Acevedo, B.P. and Fisher, H. (2013). Neural Correlates of Four Broad Temperament Dimensions:

Testing Predictions for a Novel Construct of Personality. PLoS ONE, 8.

Ekman P. (2003). Expression: Panel Discussion. Annals of the New York Academy of Sciences, 1000, 266–278. https://doi.org/10.1196/annals.1280.013

Ekman, P. (2007). Emotions Revealed (2nd Edition). Henry Holt.

Ekman P. (2016). What Scientists Who Study Emotion Agree About. Perspectives on Psychological Science: A Journal of the Association for Psychological Science, 11(1), 31–34.

Kemeny, M. E., Foltz, C., Cavanagh, J. F., Cullen, M., Giese-Davis, J., Jennings, P., Rosenberg, E. L., Gillath, O., Shaver, P. R., Wallace, B. A. and Ekman, P. (2012). Contemplative/Emotion Training Reduces Negative Emotional Behavior and Promotes Prosocial Responses. Emotion (Washington, D.C.), 12(2), 338–350. https://doi.org/10.1037/a0026118

Turan, B., Foltz, C., Cavanagh, J. F., Wallace, B. A., Cullen, M., Rosenberg, E. L., Jennings, P. A., Ekman, P. and Kemeny, M. E. (2015). Anticipatory Sensitization to Repeated Stressors: The Role of Initial Cortisol Reactivity and Meditation/Emotion Skills Training. Psychoneuroendocrinology, 52, 229–238. https://doi.org/10.1016/j.psyneuen.2014.11.014

Chapter 3. The brain and High Sensitivity

The first neuroscientific approach to try to understand specially gifted people was performed to identify the differences in intelligence. The studies were based on the idea that the size of the head could be a good indicator to explain how some individuals are more intelligent than others. It was thought that a larger greater cranial volume would certainly be an indication of greater intelligence.

Although by today's standards this may be considered an unscientific approach, it was an investigation supported by data obtained from ethology and comparative psychology, which is a branch dedicated to the study and analysis of the similarities and differences that exist between humans and other species of living beings.

Thus, it was thought that species with a larger skull, would be better prepared and adapted to their environment because they had a larger brain and therefore, would have an easier time with attentional, perceptual, or mnemonic processes and everything related to information processing.

This aspect apparently contradicted the information that came from paleontology, due to the evolution of the bone remains of the ancestors of humans, which clearly indicated an increase in the size of the skull, from Australopithecus to Homo sapiens in what has been called encephalization.

Extrapolating this vision to the animal world, it would make sense that species with a skull larger than the human skull should have a greater capacity for learning or superior abilities than humans. Such would be the case of animals like the elephant, which has the largest brain of any land-dwelling mammal.

This conclusion was partially discarded since this statement was not maintained based only on the anatomical studies of the skull, giving rise to yet another extrapolation.

The second working hypothesis, initiated during the eighties, proposed that the brains of people with greater abilities must process information or input faster than the rest of the people with a lower level of intelligence.

Based on this approach, the differences would not be found so much in the volume or structures of the brain, but in its components, that is to say, in the neurons, and more specifically in their processing speed.

Therefore, for the same cranial cavity, whoever has a greater development of brain connections would be the one who could develop more skills and abilities. This would explain why humans have greater developed abilities than other living beings with larger skulls.

The reason is that the human brain, unlike others, is structured in folds which allows it to have a greater number of neurons interconnected with each other in the same space.

High Sensitivity produces an optimization of some neuronal processes, which provides an advantage to the HSP over his or her peers in certain skills. Therefore, the advantage offered by a greater neuronal development and with better characteristics would lead to a reduction in the processing of information and interneural connections with greater intelligence as a result.

Both theories have been partially validated, thanks to the new non-invasive techniques used by neurosciences, either through the recording of brain electrical activity (EEG), or using diffusion tensor imaging (DTI), or functional magnetic resonance imaging (fMRI) among others.

Currently, it is known concerning the first hypothesis, that the importance does not lie so much in the size of the skull, nor of the brain, but in the density of the cerebral cortex, also called gray matter. In other words, the greater the number of cerebral neurons, the greater the intelligence. The data in the case of intelligence was compared using voxel-based morphometry (VBM) employing mental rotation tasks, where a rotated image is shown in different degrees to identify if it resembles the sample image. It was observed by this exercise that better performance was significantly related to a higher density of the substance in the cerebellum and other cortical regions.

Regarding the second hypothesis, which is based on processing speed, we need to keep in mind that thought as a cognitive function is supported by a biological foundation that consumes limited brain resources. The better that foundation works, the more available the resources are and a greater number of processes can happen at the same time. Likewise, a brain that is capable of utilizing its resources more efficiently will be able to respond quickly to stimuli, in that way freeing up resources for new tasks-

This hypothesis has been validated thanks to evidence from the neurosciences, by finding negative correlations between the measures of skills assessed by psychometrics, in either task resolution or tests and cortical activation during the performance of these tests.

Thus, among those with higher reading skills, a lower activation of working memory was observed compared to those with lower reading skills.

Over time, other hypotheses have emerged which complement the previous ones. For example, the diffusion tensor imaging tractography (DTI) technique is used to gather information related to the connectivity between brain regions and in white matter. This allows scientists to see a virtual dissection of the neuronal pathways in living individuals. Thanks to this technology, it has been possible to observe how at certain times there is an increase in the speed of processing. For example, at two years of age, there is an increase in synaptic connectivity and the development of myelin that surrounds the axons of nerve cells.

Research over the last decade has shown that there are significant differences and changes in the white matter, depending on the development of cognitive skills.

It must be taken into account that a cognitive function usually involves several neuronal regions, hence the importance of functional connectivity for better processing, whether it is direct communication between the cortical areas or through the corpus callosum regions.

This is something that had already been proven through the use of techniques such as fMRI by noticing an increase in associated neural pathways when developing skills such as learning to locate objects, observing an increase in functional connectivity between cortical regions associated with spatial processing, and learning the task.

Further evidence was shown in this regard with the activation of brain areas involved in a particular task, which are synchronized to work collaboratively when performing said task.

Regarding the evidence offered by the EEG used to measure the oscillation of brain wave frequencies, it has been observed how the localization of gamma wave activity (around 40 Hz) is positively related to high levels of cognitive processing, while the presence of Alpha waves (between 9 to 12 Hz) has been related to a suppression of activity.

We must take into consideration that in certain tasks, neuronal activation is as important as the suppression of other areas, since, as has been indicated, resources are limited. Therefore, the key to optimizing the performance of a task is to use the resources solely on that task, suppressing any other activity until it is finished.

One of the most curious phenomena presented in recent years about intelligence and its relationship with the brain has to do with what has been called the default mode network (DMN), which refers to what the brain does while it is not doing any particular task as opposed to when it is doing something, which is called a task-positive network (TPN). It has been noted that there are differences in the default mode network in patients with schizophrenia, autism, or Alzheimer's disease, although its implications in these cases remain unclear.

Regarding intelligence, they found that the DMN correlates positively and significantly with the results of intelligence tests, that is, the brains of individuals who have more capacity remain more active even at rest compared to those of the rest of the people.

Neuroscience has made it possible to observe neuronal differences between teachers and learners on a given subject. It has also made it possible for scientists to observe how the brain changes, specializing neuronal groups for the performance of tasks that previously were not performed.

This has been verified by magnetoencephalography (MEG), which is used to analyze the relationship between neural structures and their function, how changes in the motor cortex occur in the area responsible for the fingers, one of the first pieces of evidence of neural plasticity, thanks to the continuous practice of an activity as it is the case of when a person goes from learning to play the violin to teaching how to play the violin.

But these neuronal differences do not only affect learning. It has also been found that it makes the person more sensitive to stimulation, for example, the auditory, responding more intensely to sound, both in its amplitude and duration. This type of hypersensitivity has also been observed in the rest of the senses: vision, touch, taste, or smell.

Special mention should be made of the emotional brain of particularly gifted people, where it has been observed that they tend to have greater connectivity between the anterior cingulate cortex and the frontal cortex. This explains their great curiosity and also their differential emotional processing, showing hypersensitivity to emotions including the suffering of symptoms associated with depression or anxiety.

But these are not the only brain changes found, since, thanks to neuronal plasticity, each individual can "mold" his brain differently from the rest. However, there are great similarities between individuals due to their exposure to common experiences offered by a shared culture. A very recent study by Sarah Pierce and colleagues (2021) corroborates the existence of facts that provide information about neural underpinnings of the differences in sensory processing sensitivity present in different groups of individuals.

In the case of Highly Sensitive people, research supports the depth of cognitive processing, which is as much of a determining feature in the trait of high sensitivity as it is difficult to perceive at first sight. The review of scientific studies on the brain and High Sensitivity by Greven et al. (2019) indicates that the combination of human and animal research allows major advances to be made in understanding the mechanism underlying the highly sensitive trait. Human research highlights facets of the trait in the highly sensitive person, because they are highly intuitive, can easily integrate information, and respond to the affective states of others close to them, highlighting depth of processing, awareness of subtleties, and empathy for others. On the other hand, animal research allows us to control for environmental factors and provides information on behavioral patterns, such as those related to boldness, proactive behavior, cautiousness, extroversion, or introversion.

FRAN 47 YEARS OLD

Fran is a 47-year-old journalist who has just started a new relationship after eight years of his previous engagement. Fran likes quiet places, nature, and even shopping on days when it's not too busy. Mayka, his new partner, is an attorney, a little younger than Fran. She loves busy shopping days, Black Friday shopping, and any other busy holiday shopping day. Something was wrong in the relationship that required them to go see a psychologist and start couple's therapy.

There was physical attraction and full sexual satisfaction in the relationship. Since the problem was occurring in the initial phase of the relationship, the possibility that the cause was due to wear and tear or the presence of more attractive alternatives were ruled out. Cognitive phenomena such as assumptions or expectations were also not very relevant to the problem. Everything pointed more to individual differences between the couple. Mayka was a very practical girl, while Fran was very analytical. Both had communication and conflict resolution skills, which would make it easier to achieve the objectives in psychological therapy. The goal was to help them both to have a much more rewarding relationship with each other. It would be possible if we managed to encourage and adjust these two behaviors, communication and ability to solve critical situations.

Continuing with the evaluation of the couple, the Lopez-Altschwager problem questionnaire (adapted from Hahlweg, Revenstorf & Schindler, 1984) was used to assess some aspects that could pose problems both as a couple and individuals. Likewise, the HSP test available on the web at https://pasespana.com/test-personas-altamente-sensibles (in Spanish) used to detect highly sensitive people, was necessary due to Fran's personality characteristics. Individual interviews were then conducted with each member of the couple separately. It was essential to obtain information about the past, present, and future of the relationship between Fran and Mayka. As a final part of the evaluation process, a round table was proposed, before the counseling sessions.

As expected, Fran was an HSP. The trait of high sensitivity that had accompanied him all his life and had never given him any problems was now noticeable and impactful in his relationship with Mayka. She had a personality that was entirely different and opposite to Fran's. However, their mutual knowledge of each other's temperamental factors helped them to make a success of the therapy. Counseling in positive reciprocity, communication, negotiation, and conflict resolution, were adapted taking into account that Fran is a highly sensitive person. The result was positive thanks to the mutual respect and the love they had for each other. Couples therapy worked, they managed to be happy together despite their differences.

References

Belsky, J. (1997). Variation in Susceptibility to Environmental Influence: An Evolutionary Argument. Psychological Inquiry, 8(3), 182-186. Retrieved May 29, 2021.

Borries F. (2012). Do the "Highly Sensitive" Exist? A Taxonometric Investigation of the Personality Construct Sensory Processing Sensitivity. Ph.D. Thesis (unpublished doctoral dissertation), Univ. Bielefeld.

Déry, M., Lapalme, M., Jagiellowicz, J., Poirier, M., Temcheff, C. and Toupin, J. (2017). Predicting Depression and Anxiety from Oppositional Defiant Disorder Symptoms in Elementary School-Age Girls and Boys with Conduct Problems. Child Psychiatry and Human Development, 48(1), 53–62. https://doi.org/10.1007/s10578-016-0652-5

Ellis, B. J., Boyce, W. T., Belsky, J., Bakermans-Kranenburg, M. J. and van Ijzendoorn, M. H. (2011). Differential Susceptibility to the Environment: An Evolutionary-Neurodevelopmental Theory. Dev. Psychopathol. 23, 7–28.

Hahlweg, K., Revenstorf, D. and Schindler, L. (1984). Effects of Behavioral Marital Therapy on Couples' Communication and Problem-Solving Skills. Journal of Consulting and Clinical Psychology, 52(4), 553–566. https://doi.org/10.1037/0022-006X.52.4.553

Greven, C. U., Lionetti, F., Booth, C., Aron, E. N., Fox, E., Schendan, H. E., Homberg, J. (2019). Sensory Processing Sensitivity in the Context of Environmental Sensitivity: A Critical Review and Development of Research Agenda. Neuroscience and Biobehavioral Reviews, 98, 287–305.

Jagiellowicz, J., Xu, X., Aron, A., Aron, E., Cao, G., Feng, T. and Weng, X. (2011). The Trait of Sensory Processing Sensitivity and Neural Responses to Changes in Visual Scenes. Social Cognitive and Affective Neuroscience, 6(1), 38–47. https://doi.org/10.1093/scan/nsq001

Jagiellowicz, J., Zarinafsar, S. and Acevedo, B.P. (2020). Health and Social Outcomes in Highly Sensitive Persons.

Lionetti, F., Aron, A., Aron, E. N., Burns, G. L., Jagiellowicz, J. and Pluess, M. (2018). Dandelions, Tulips, and Orchids: Evidence for the Existence of Low-sensitive, Medium-sensitive, and High-sensitive individuals. Translational Psychiatry, 8(1), 24. https://doi.org/10.1038/s41398-017-0090-6

Pierce, S., Kadlaskar, G., Edmondson, D.A. et al. Associations Between Sensory Processing and

Electrophysiological and Neurochemical Measures in Children with ASD: An EEG-MRS study. Journal of Neurodevelopmental Disorders 13, 5 (2021). https://doi.org/10.1186/s11689-020-09351-0

48

Chapter 4. Non-sensitive and Sensitive Patients

When we talk about sensitivity, more than likely we all think in degrees. We may also think that a very sensitive person is hypersensitive. Therefore, it is important to define our terms. Hypersensitivity refers to a dangerous overreaction to an external agent, such as a virus, bacteria, or allergen. There is no reason why being hypersensitive should be related to being an HSP. Hypersensitive people suffer from a medical condition that prevents them from controlling the reaction that their body experiences. On the other hand, for the HSP, reacting in a more exaggerated way to certain sensations or external agents is a matter of perception. The reaction has nothing to do with allergies or toxins. We could define it as an intense and peculiar way of perceiving, which can become annoying or even manifest itself as hypochondria.

Generally, the majority, approximately 80% of the population, are not bothered by noise, fluorescent lights, or other stimulating elements in the environment. Most people don't stop to think that they are bothered by the volume of the car radio. Most people don't need to suddenly turn off the television because they are disturbed by the hum. Most people just turn off the radio if they're not interested in the topic and turn off the TV if they're not watching. Experiences that involve a sudden change don't have to be over-stimulating, they can change a plan at the last minute without drama. The visual stimulation that video games, television advertising, and going to the movies transmit to us is usually a source of enjoyment. Going to shopping malls, basketball games or the local fair is a leisure activity most look forward to. Depending on their tastes, most people are interested in dramatic, horror, or violent films and they can at least watch them just for the sake of entertainment. This is why they are surprised when they see the HSP cry when watching a dramatic movie. Dramatic movies are just another genre in the regular repertoire of any non-HSP person because it does not even cross their mind that they can't watch such films because of how it is going to affect them.

Knowing how another person feels, what they think, and how they perceive situations is a challenge for most people. But for the HSP who is capable of perceiving other people's feelings beyond purely objective vision, this comes naturally. Everyone can remember a time when someone has noticed how you feel without giving you any information. It is about non-verbal language, HSPs due to their depth of processing, can perceive emotions that at first glance are not seen. The person who is feeling them does not intend to manifest them, but leaves some kind of trace or signal easily detected by the HSP. Highly sensitive people, being a minority in society, soon begin to notice that they are different from others. In addition, they can detect when other people also belong to this approximate twenty percent of the population. Sometimes the HSP feels misunderstood because they are a minority. As for the others, approximately eighty percent of the population is the majority. It is difficult for them to acquire the ability to put themselves in the shoes of a highly sensitive person, especially if they are not aware of the characteristics of the trait, especially if we are talking about a layperson in psychology, or if they are a person with little empathy, or just by nature, unable to put themselves in the other person's shoes.

Regarding the future, non-HSP people do not tend to generate cause-effect anticipatory thinking. They live more in the present unless they suffer from a pathological mental disorder. Under normal conditions, they go about their lives without much regard for the consequences, at least those that do not involve important decisions. That is, they can make plans for the weekend as a matter of course without thinking immediately if it will be cold, or if they will meet a person who is in a bad mood, or not remembering the times when similar plans didn't quite work out. They simply live, act and perform actions with all the naturalness in the world. They act without the need to generate in their mind an accumulation of possibilities, precautions, or contradictions. They also don't have as many medical tests and tend to take risks without taking as many precautions. When they make mistakes, they try a second time immediately, without generating a ruminative thought of reflection to change the strategy of the attempt. Their nature does not demand that they immediately assess all the mistakes that have arisen in the past in similar situations. Nor does it prevent them from acting out of prudence as to what might happen.

It can be a challenge for the HSP to achieve an acceptable level of stimulation in the workplace. Also, it is a challenge for them to find enjoyable places of leisure. It is common that at first, they may feel uncomfortable because of the elements of the environment, but their creativity will make them keep air freshener in their desk drawer for the smells that may come from the pipes, a cardigan for when the central air conditioning season begins, or always carry a bottle of water or candy for when they have dry mouth. Many are relieved to discover that they are an HSP after having lived a life they can only describe as full of suffering. A life in which they did not understand what was happening to them. Wondering all the time before discovering High Sensitivity, why so much intolerance, or why they have not been able to feel good in certain places or situations.

Concerning children, the differences also begin to be noticed from a very early age. On the one hand, we have those who present the trait of high sensitivity, as opposed to the majority who do not present it. Behaviors that they perform unconsciously, as a result of their nature, can be considered manifestations of leadership in some populations or they may be categorized as odd or bizarre behavior elsewhere. Respecting that we are all the same, but with different needs may be the key to success for everyone. To be able to accept the trait of high sensitivity as one more way of feeling and, therefore, just another way of behaving.

References

Acevedo, B.P. (2020). The Basics of Sensory Processing Sensitivity.

Belsky, J. and Pluess, M. The Nature (and Nurture?) of Plasticity in Early Human Development. Perspect. Psychol. Sci. 4, 345–351 (2009).

Belsky J. and Pluess M. (2016) Developmental Psychopathology (ed Cicchetti, D.) 3rd Edition, Vol 3, p 59.

Dispenza M. C. (2019). Classification of Hypersensitivity Reactions. Allergy and Asthma Proceedings, 40(6), 470–473. https://doi.org/10.2500/aap.2019.40.4274

Hefferon, K. and Pluess, M. (2013). Genetics and Wellbeing. Hefferon, K., Positive Psychology and the Body: the Somatopsychic side of Flourishing. New York, NY: McGraw-Hill.

Hillert, L., and Kolmodin-Hedman, B. (1997). Hypersensitivity to Electricity: Sense or Sensibility?. Journal of Psychosomatic Research, 42(5), 427–432. https://doi.org/10.1016/s0022-3999(96)00374-1

McKay, D. and Acevedo, B.P. (2020). Clinical Characteristics of Misophonia and its Relation to Sensory Processing Sensitivity: A Critical Analysis.

Meyer, B., Muriel, A. and David, P. B. (2005). Sensory Sensitivity, Attachment Experiences, and Rejection Responses Among Adults with Borderline and Avoidant Personality Features. J. Personal. Disord. 19, 641–658.

Smolewska, K. A., McCabe, S. B. and Woody, E. Z. (2006). A Psychometric Evaluation of the Highly Sensitive Person Scale: The Components of Sensory-Processing Sensitivity and their Relation to the BIS/BAS and "Big Five". Pers. Individ. Dif. 40, 1269–1279.

Woolcock A. J. (1976). Immediate Hypersensitivity: A Clinical Review. Australian and New Zealand Journal of Medicine, 6(2), 158–167. https://doi.org/10.1111/j.1445-5994.1976.tb03313

56

Chapter 5. Education. High Capacity and High Sensitivity

Students in school are grouped according to chronological age. However, during the first years of a person's life, other criteria stand out in which we could make classifications. In reality, it is about mental age and emotional age. As the individual grows older, under normal conditions, the three types of age balance each other out. The difference lies in the pace of learning a particular skill, but not in the development of that skill. For example, some children begin to speak later in life, but end up having an excellent command of language. Some children start walking later than others but end up being great athletes.

As they grow up, children with high capacities maintain that difference that characterizes them between their chronological age and their mental age, or between their emotional age and their mental age. In comparison with other children of the same chronological age, the level of intellectual, social, and emotional development stands out. To identify high ability within their peer group, we look at their need to imagine, create or investigate. Because they are self-motivated, they can reason and communicate in a more advanced way. In addition to all this, there is greater sensitivity in those who qualify as more capable. High Intellectual Ability is therefore a multidimensional phenomenon that includes specific talent and unique personality characteristics, including moral sensitivity.

In this sense, the characteristics in common between highly sensitive people and people with high capacities lie both in their creativity and emotional intensity. Both types of people may require special educational needs to promote their abilities.

Once adulthood arrives, both personality types are characterized by being very competent in certain professions, such as teachers, psychologists, or nurses. They stand out for their creativity, empathy, or altruism.

To date, it has been observed how individuals with sensory processing sensitivity (SPS) may show anatomical and connectivity differences at the neural level. The expression of these differences is manifested through cognitive processing. All this allows us to understand that it is a "different mind" because in this way the highly sensitive person can process a greater amount of information, separating the irrelevant, accessing more data than previously recorded. All this is done at the same time, thanks to their unique working memory, with the addition of metacognition, which supervises the whole procedure, detecting and correcting errors, thus optimizing the final result.

This is a condition that can be observed as early as childhood, although there is some controversy about its diagnosis because it can sometimes lead to a certain degree of social stigma, especially due to the lack of knowledge of some aspects in the general population.

From neuro-constructivism, development is conceived as a succession of orderly changes throughout life in which gene expression is combined through epigenesis, brain structure, and functioning, with cognitive processes, thus forming a unique individual.

The sensitive intelligence that characterizes both people with high abilities and HSPs sometimes creates an educational need. This poses a growing demand in schools and families. Achieving equal opportunities will mean that sensitive talents will be able to reach their maximum personal development.

To the extent that educational programs take into account the characteristics of HSC, each of them will be able to stand out. The system and the individuals around these children will be helping them to enhance their development. In this way, the environment will play a decisive role as an intermediary in the development of individual skills.

On the other hand, other approaches extend the intervention of the environment beyond school by including both family and friends in their models. For these models, it is necessary not only to intervene at an academic level but also to try to offer the appropriate environmental conditions to facilitate the development of the highly sensitive child.

HSPs may be more vulnerable to suffering from a temporary disorder at some point in their lives. They are born with an innate temperament and the environment shapes their personality. An environment filled with excessive or stressful stimuli can become a focus of susceptibility for the HSP. On the contrary, an environment with positive stimuli and in line with the HSP personality provides the right circumstances to live in harmony with their trait. Achieving a balance between trait and environment will be the key to personal growth and educational and professional success.

References

Dabrowski, K. (1972). Psychoneurosis Is Not an Illness. Gryf Publications.

Piechowski, M. M. (1979). Developmental Potential. N. Colangelo and R. T. Zaffrann (eds): New Voices Counseling the Gifted. Dubuque, IA: Kendall/Hunt, 25-57.

Piechowski, M. M. (1980). Emotional Sources of Intellectual Well-being. Dissertation presented at the American Educational Research Association Annual Meeting, April 7-11.

Piechowski, M. M. and Colangelo, N. (1984). Developmental Potential of the Gifted. Gifted Child Quarterly 28, 80-88.

Piechowski, M. M., Falk, F. and Silverman, L. K. (1986). Comparison of Intellectually and Artistically Gifted on Five Dimensions of Mental Functioning. Perceptual and Motor Skills 60, 539-549.

Piechowski, M. M. (1986). The Concept of Developmental Potential. Roeper Review 8 (3), 190-197.

Silverman, L. K. (1996). The Emotional Needs of the Gifted. AGATE: Journal of the Gifted and Talented, Education Council of the Alberta Teachers' Association 10 (2), 2-15.

Silverman. L. K. (2002). Upside-down Brilliance: The Visual-Spatial Learner. Denver: DeLeon Publishing.

Silverman, L. K. (2018). Assessment of Giftedness. S. Pfeiffer (Ed.), Handbook of Giftedness in Children: Educational Theory, Research, and Best Practices (2nd ed., pp.183-207). New York: Springer Science.

Silverman, W. K., Albano, A. M. and Sandín, B. (2001). Interview for the Diagnosis of Anxiety Disorders in Children According to DSM-IV. ADIS-IV: C. Child's Interview. Madrid: Klinik.

Chapter 6. Differentiating Characteristics of Highly Sensitive People

6.1. Is High Sensitivity a disorder?

The American Psychiatric Association (APA) is the author of the basic diagnostic textbook that serves as a guide for professionals. The Diagnostic and Statistical Manual of Mental Disorders (DSM) defines "disorder" as a behavioral and psychological pattern associated with present distress or disability. As well as a significantly increased risk of pain, death or significant loss of freedom as a manifestation of dysfunction.

A highly sensitive person may be distressed (feeling different), run the risk of falling into depression or anxiety (due to ruminative thinking), experience a sense of loss of freedom to participate in certain situations (due to inability to be in crowded places), or suffer from their own reactions to culturally unacceptable situations (need for time alone). All these peculiar behavioral and psychological manifestations could be interpreted as symptoms of a disorder. It has even been interpreted this way when the existence of the highly sensitive trait was not known.

According to Elaine Aron these and similar behaviors have been interpreted as expected in 15% of the population. We take into account both its advantages and disadvantages. The position of viewing attitudes and manifestations of the HSP trait as a disorder is becoming increasingly unacceptable among psychology specialists, psychiatrists, or school counselors, even among the individuals who are HSP, although they go to the doctor for help and the parents who go to the school counselor for answers. At first, it is easy to think that what bothers you may be a dysfunction. But in reality, these behaviors are normal, they are just different.

Highly sensitive people who are aware of the trait no longer see the presence of these symptoms as a disadvantage, although they may feel hurt by the disapproving response of the people around them. Such a response is often perceived in environments where the trait is unfamiliar. Distinguishing temperament in general from disorders is a challenge in our society. Especially if we are talking about children, who are the most defenseless group in this respect.

When the highly sensitive person goes to a specialist seeking help, they will exhibit extreme behavior. The usual thing is to show the psychologist what is hurting them and what they blame as the source of their discomfort. That is the feature of the trait based on the depth of processing, analyzing everything before acting, as well as processing future alternatives and their consequences and the time this requires. Needless to say, all this can become an impediment when it comes to expressing or manifesting what the person really wants to say.

Social skills are learned through experience. Some people acquire them immediately at an early age and others may even go to a psychologist to learn them. But for HSPs and HSC the high levels of arousal, due to their innate trait, can lead them to distort their true behavior. This behavior will be addressed in these first interactions with the specialist, both because of fear of criticism, the culturally acquired shame towards their trait, as well as the awareness of their defects.

Anyone outside of an optimal level of comfort will underperform the task at hand. This becomes evident in communication between non-peers for example, when a patient talks to his psychologist or a parent trying to communicate with the school counselor, or even more so if we are talking about child-adult communication. This is the case when a highly sensitive child tries to seek help for emotional distress, whether they go to their teacher, their school counselor or their parent, poor communication performance in the initial stages may be interpreted by the listener as low intelligence, anxiety, shyness, avoidance, verbal aggression, or a personality disorder.

In addition to the confusion that can occur in the initial moments, the great misunderstanding that worries professionals and parents is in the misdiagnosis. There are many cases of highly sensitive people, but they have been diagnosed with a disorder. On the other hand, some who do suffer from a mental disorder, prefer to think that they are just very sensitive. And, thirdly, there are cases of people who in addition to having a disorder, are highly sensitive. Disorders with which high sensitivity can be confused range from intellectual disability. ADHD, or autism spectrum disorders.

6.2. Autism and High Sensitivity

In clinical practice, we may find people who are highly sensitive, who are are more vulnerable to depression or anxiety especially if they have had a bad upbringing, the same as would happen to someone who is not sensitive. On the other hand, some highly sensitive people never develop any disorders but they have been diagnosed with one. Just as some people are diagnosed as highly sensitive when in reality they suffer from some type of disorder.

Specific DSM diagnoses, such as autism spectrum, could lead to confusion with high sensitivity. Many autistic people are distressed by high levels of specific types of stimulation. At the same time, they may ignore other body language or signs in their environment, such as social cues.

Leo Kanner (1943) described the autistic disorder as "Lack of contact with people, self-absorption and emotional loneliness." We could say that the autistic spectrum is a psychological disorder characterized by a person's intense concentration on his or her inner world and the progressive loss of contact with external reality. It is characterized by severe, permanent, and profound developmental deficits that affect socialization, communication, imagination, and behavior, among other things.

People with autism have high sensitivity due to poor use of sensory information and not at all due to the deep processing of information, as happens to people defined as highly sensitive. High levels of stimulation turn into confusion or even violence in people with autism. Through the instruction of their educators, new habits, and distractions are created to correct disruptive behaviors. Highly sensitive people, on the other hand, can tolerate high levels of stimulation. They increasingly adjust to the appropriate way to reduce such stimulation employing a maturational learning process.

A characteristic of highly sensitive people is a high level of empathy as well as excellent social skills, especially in family environments. Often in a consultation, we observe a marked improvement in some of the signs of behavior, communication, or sociability in the youngest children. Signs that at first seemed like items consistent with a disorder. Generating a familiar, comfortable, playful, and sensitive environment helps us to observe in order to evaluate more accurately the initial symptoms thus avoiding misdiagnosis.

Occupational Therapists work with children who have learning or behavioral problems due to poor sensory integration. These are children who have a deficit in the ability of the central nervous system to interpret and organize the information received by the various sense organs. This information, received by the brain, is analyzed and used to allow contact with the environment and to respond appropriately. Highly sensitive people, on the other hand, are more impacted by sensory input such as bright lights, loud noises, smells, or rough textures. They come from the processing of stimuli, not from the sense organ itself.

High sensitivity is an innate trait, a normal variation of temperament, not a mental disorder. Some highly sensitive people have diagnosable disorders, although most do not. The same way happens to some people who are not highly sensitive. These individuals may or may not have diagnosable disorders. Highly sensitive people respond well to treatments for sensory integration disorder. However, the characteristics of their innate trait cannot entirely be eliminated.

Improving knowledge about the trait that highly sensitive people possess makes it easier for them to learn ways to adapt to life. No treatment will eliminate the innate trait, which can be an advantage in certain contexts. The strategy of managing the highly sensitive person must be based on the promotion of the qualities he or she possesses and in the positive reformulation of their characteristics, adapting them to the environment for optimal development of their personality.

Mental health professionals find that full disclosure is necessary to avoid diagnostic confusion. They also involve the rest of the family in counseling to learn how to resolve conflicts that may arise during the childhood of a highly sensitive person.

6.3. Attention Deficit Hyperactivity Disorder and High Sensitivity

Highly sensitive people, when overstimulated, may appear agitated, hyperactive, or unfocused. On the other hand, they show good attention and calmness when the stimulation of the environment is optimal for them. In children, their reaction to over-stimulation can lead to the belief that they have Attention Deficit Hyperactivity Disorder (ADHD). That's why so many parents test their children for this disorder. In reality, far fewer children suffer from it after all.

People with Attention Deficit Disorder (ADD) have difficulties in other aspects of learning. Problems with emotional regulation, social functioning, or behavior. People who suffer from this chronic deterioration in their ability to pay attention may appear as lacking self-will, but that is not the reality. Many parents ask the psychologist to explain how it is possible that their child can pay attention when engaged in what interests him/her and at the same time be incapable of attending to school tasks or rules that do not provide a motivating stimulus. This is precisely what it means to suffer from ADD. It is an "unconscious helplessness" in the face of tasks that are not intrinsically motivating. It is something much more complex than a simple lack of concentration.

ADD is not simply an excessive distraction. It includes a chronic failure to engage in academic tasks. Some examples are, leaving things for later, poor planning of activities, avoidance of that which involves a sustained mental effort, or losing the pace assigned to them in class.

Brown (2006), professor of psychiatry at Yale University, speaks of ADD as a complex disorder. It involves impairment of concentration, organization, motivation, emotional modulation, memory, and other functions of the brain's control system. What we pay attention to depends on what we perceive, remember, think, do, and even feel. People with ADHD sometimes demonstrate a mood similar to boredom, lack of motivation, irritability, or lack of control when faced with frustration, in addition to feeling overwhelmed or stressed.

Corral (2005), indicates that in the brain of children with ADHD there may be low activity in the frontal lobes and limbic system, related to the attentional system, after observation by positron emission tomography (PET). Likewise, through magnetic resonance imaging (MRI) it has been discovered that they have lower levels of dopamine, a neurotransmitter that allows communication between various structures of the brain. The conclusion is that these brain disorders can be aggravated if there are other factors, such as family conflicts or lack of parental educational skills.

Highly sensitive children may have symptoms similar to those of children with ADHD. In both cases, abnormal behaviors may appear, such as not being able to entertain themselves with anything, continually demanding parental attention, lack of control of emotions, or difficulty in maintaining motivation towards certain tasks. Establishing a clinical diagnosis of ADHD and a differential diagnosis concerning High Sensitivity is the most efficient way to avoid confusion.

GONZALO 3 YEARS OLD

Gonzalo was only three and a half years old when his parents brought him in for a consultation because they were worried about the constant complaints they were receiving from his first year's kindergarten teacher. The little boy showed restlessness in class, he did not pay attention when the teacher spoke, everything was a game to him. At home, there were constant arguments due to the different parenting styles that each parent employed. The father was very flexible, he allowed Gonzalo to do everything, he said that his son knew how to behave well when he wanted to and when he felt good. On the other hand, the mother set all the rules and applied harsh discipline, with constant scolding, small threats, and punishments. After interviewing the parents and examining the child, characteristics consistent with having the trait of high sensitivity were observed. At the same time, however, there was much to be done to rule out the possibility of ADHD.

After the initial stage of evaluation and observation, the following therapeutic intervention objectives were set: improve attention span, work on cognitive and mastery skills to facilitate learning (perception, memory, organization, classification, etc.) as well as the promotion of social skills with peers. At the same time, sessions were held with parents to establish consensual educational guidelines according to their child's personality traits. By the end of treatment, Gonzalo had been brought up to standards both at school and at home. He had also improved his self-esteem and was more tolerant of frustration. His sense of accomplishment in the tasks he performed and in his relationship with peers generated greater independence in his behavior. Months went by and the achievements made by the child were maintained. The initial symptoms that pointed to ADHD had completely disappeared.

References:

Cattell, R. B. (1973). Personality and Mood by Questionnaire. Jossey-Bass Publishers.

Cattell, R. B. and Meredith, G. M. (1976). Psychological Theories of Personality. Editorial Paidós.

Eysenck, H. J. (1965). Extraversion and the Acquisition of Eyeblink and GSR -Conditioned Responses. Psychological Bulletin, 63(4), 258–270 https://doi.org/10.1037/h0021921

Eysenck, H. J. and Eysenck, S. G. B. (1965). The Eysenck Personality Inventory. British Journal of Educational Studies, 14, 140–140.

Jagiellowicz, J., Aron, A., Aron, E.N. (2016). Relation Between the Temperament Trait of Sensory Processing Sensitivity and Emotional Reactivity. Social Behavior and Personality, 44 (2), 185-200.

Kanner L (1943) Autistic Disturbances of Affective Contact. The Nervous Child 2:217–250.

Monjas Casares. M. I. (2004). Is My Child Shy? Editorial Pirámide.

Monjas, I. and Caballo, V. E. (2002). Psychopathology and Treatment of Shyness in Childhood. Caballo and Simón (Eds.), Handbook of Clinical Child and Adolescent Psychology (pp. 271-296). Editorial Pirámide.

Pluess, M., Assary E, Lionetti F, Lester K, Krapohl E, Aron E. and Aron, A. (2018) Environmental Sensitivity in Children: Development of the Highly Sensitive Child Scale and Identification of Sensitivity Groups. Developmental Psychology. https://doi.org/10.1037/dev0000406

Suomi, S. J. (1991). Up-tight and Laid-back Monkeys: Individual Differences in the Response to Social Challenges. S. Brauth, W. Hall and R. Dooling (Eds.), Plasticity of Development. MIT Press. https://doi.org/10.1093/oxfordjournals.bmb.a011598.

78

Chapter 7. Effects of High Sensitivity

7.1. Fear of failure of the highly sensitive person

When people come in for a consultation and they put their fears on the table, it is not always easy to help them see their life in a positive light. On the other hand, when dealing with highly sensitive people, the task of making them reflect on their actions is quite simple. It is an advantage to deal with an HSP, thanks to the ability they have to observe the subtleties of each situation, deeply analyze the information, and the memory they possess, among other qualities. They remember many details and even recall dreams from their childhood.

We know that it is their nervous system that leads them to think and act in this unique and different way. It makes them thoughtful, intuitive, and creative; it also makes them feel things intensely, and enables them to predict outcomes. They care about social justice and the feelings of others. In therapy, they show their understanding of the mistakes they have made, and perhaps eliminating guilt is the key to beginning psychological treatment with an HSP. They know what their mistakes are and recognizing them can be a good start to successful therapy.

When the trait begins to interfere with their environment, potentially harming the individual, it is time to ask for help or go to psychotherapy.

We have seen how the development of the highly sensitive person influences his trait, finding advantages or disadvantages. The influence of the environment is not unique to HSC. Even the classical authors of psychology books have demonstrated how the environment influences a child's behavior. Perhaps the difference lies in the intensity of the emotions and the depth of information processing.

The HSC (highly sensitive children) who come to psychotherapy show us every day how intensely they respond to situations that generate positive emotions. For example, they respond excellently to rewards when positive reinforcement or token economy are implemented.

In the same way that it would be a simplistic definition to use the term "prone to obesity" as the only characteristic to define people with a high-calorie diet, it would be very just as simplistic to consider high sensitivity as high vulnerability or propensity to negative affect, since we would only be talking about specific cases. However, many highly sensitive people do not experience these negative symptoms. Although there is a significant amount of consultation data, we cannot have statistical data on the rest of the people who do not go for a consultation.

In this sense, an impairment is considered pathological when it occurs in all contexts, for example, a hyperactive child is hyperactive at home, at school, and his grandparents' house, or wherever he goes.

Cognitive-behavioral treatment is used in clinical practice to address childhood problems such as shyness. The first step is to contextualize the reality of each HSC in question, as each child is unique and each experience is different. HSCs have their trait characteristics in common but differ in the type of parenting they receive and in the variability of other personality factors. After an initial assessment of the child and his or her family and school environment, the learning of social skills and behavior modification will be the starting point of the process to eliminate the withdrawal behavior that is interfering with the child's well-being.

The greatest asset we have is our life, but we find more and more people who feel they have no life of their own, people who feel manipulated by others or are victims of their experiences.

Many people sometimes become their own worst enemy, meaning that they elaborate a ruminative thought process based on the analysis of a situation they have experienced and generate feelings of guilt and emotional discomfort. Other people allow themselves to be continually manipulated to the point of losing their own identity for fear of failing and not being the ideal daughter, sister, partner, or friend.

Highly sensitive people must learn to set boundaries, say "no" at the right time, and let themselves be guided by their intuition to recognize those people who bring them enriching relationships and to avoid those who they feel create toxic relationships.

Something necessary to survive in a world where HSPs are a minority is to be able to make decisions without fear of not being perfect even if those decisions have a negative effect on other people. Likewise, it is necessary to have good self-esteem to be happy, learn the necessary skills to communicate what you want and feel, and put yourself first as long as it doesn't harm the other person.

7.2. Pathological self-criticism of the highly sensitive person

To correct this behavior, psychologists use treatments against anticipatory anxiety and to solve previous negative expectations, which the patient generates repeatedly and automatically.

Anxiety is understood as a situation of excessive and disproportionate distress and fear in everyday situations that can produce feelings of paralysis and helplessness. Many who suffer from anxiety can identify with at least one or all of the following statements:

Throughout the day I often find myself in a situation of tension, nervousness, or agitation.

I often have feelings of panic with a sense of impending danger.

Sometimes I feel my heart pounding and my breathing quicken for no apparent reason.

Sometimes I am in a state of restlessness that prevents me from remaining at rest without moving.

Research indicates that highly sensitive people are more vulnerable to anxiety, especially when they have had difficult childhoods. We understand difficult childhoods as those based on unstructured family and social environments. But people who, because they are highly sensitive, feel different and misunderstood, even under a healthy and seemingly balanced upbringing, can also develop some form of anxiety disorder. For a highly sensitive person, the greatest predictor of pathological anxiety is having experienced acute or cumulative emotional trauma, with the person's inner world being responsible for determining whether or not such trauma appears.

Orgiles, Espada, and Mendez (2005) talk about anxiety as an emotion that is inherent to all people. The body tends to react with an activation of the autonomic nervous system to those stimuli that may pose a threat, providing an adaptive or survival response in the person who is undergoing such a situation. However, when this emotion becomes extreme, it can be categorized as an anxiety disorder that manifests itself when there is intense anxiety triggered by a situation where there is no sufficient reason to generate an alarm. In these situations with no real cause for alarm, anxiety loses its adaptive value and causes discomfort in the individual, interfering with the normal performance of daily activities.

Bados (2010) indicates that the most common areas of worry that characterize Generalized Anxiety Disorder are usually related to daily life, such as family, friends, money, work, or health. It is considered that social concerns may have even more weight than the rest of the concerns. In general, there is no difference in the content of what worries people with and without an anxiety disorder, but the former worry more about minor issues.

Therefore, in adults, we find that they manifest anxiety disorder when they are worried about things that in reality will never happen, are very unlikely to happen, or are not as dramatic as they perceive them to be. In the person who suffers from anxiety, a chain of negative and constant thoughts is produced, which are practically uncontrollable and are oriented towards a future danger. HSPs may be more predisposed to anxiety as a disorder due to their cognitive tendency to mull over new or what they perceive as threatening situations. When anxiety goes from being something natural for survival to becoming a disorder, the individual becomes unable to find solutions no matter how many times he/she thinks about it. This renders them unable to make decisions, generating a tendency to worry about mistakes and failures persistently.

Children's reactions to anxiety symptoms are significantly different from those of adults, leading to negative consequences that can interfere with their growth and maturation. Certain events can trigger anxiety in children, from the birth of a sibling, the start of school, or a change of address. Some of the child anxiety problems that are a common reason for visiting psychologists and psychiatrists due to their importance and/or severity are generalized anxiety, separation anxiety, panic disorder, post-traumatic stress disorder, and obsessive-compulsive disorder.

Generalized anxiety disorder is characterized by the persistence of frequent worries that the individual associates with something negative that he/she thinks is going to happen, usually related to a traumatic event he/she has experienced. For highly sensitive people it is easier for an event to become traumatic due to their propensity for taking emotions to the extreme automatically. Taking into account that their innate trait makes them feel both positive and negative emotions intensely.

In children, parenting can also play a role, as an overprotective or demanding parenting style can lead to insecure attachment, giving them wrong expectations about their ability to deal with negative events and preventing them from developing the necessary skills to solve problematic situations. HSC, possessing increased attention due to their depth of cognitive processing, may generate an attentional bias or hypervigilance to stimuli that they consider threatening, generating excessive worries that may prevent them from focusing on other tasks.

For example, interpreting a teacher's gaze as negative can cause an HSC to have high levels of anxiety and worry thinking that he/she has done something wrong. The highly sensitive child analyzes in-depth the effects of the situation. In this case, to reduce anxiety, the child seeks strategies such as remaining constantly alert to the teacher's behavior or avoiding going to school in his or her efforts to avoid the discomfort in the short term. However, this contributes to the development of an anxiety disorder and generates additional problems.

In a society like ours, in which both adults and children live immersed in continuous changes, new projects, and numerous activities, sometimes it is difficult to distinguish whether we are feeling the natural anxiety of survival, or we are at the beginning of an anxiety disorder, especially for those who are the most susceptible to it such as HSPs and HSC.

Regarding the treatment for anxiety disorder, it should be based on two main areas, improving stress through relaxation techniques, as well as combating frequent worries, for which the psychologist will use cognitive restructuring techniques, self-guiding, and graded exposure. Some specialists opt for non-directive therapies, based on helping the patient to understand their feelings clearly, to understand themselves better, and to be able to discover for themselves what they can do to change what they feel and what is causing them discomfort.

7.3. Depression vs. High Sensitivity

Depression is understood to be a feeling of constant sadness that generates hopelessness, irritability, and discomfort in daily personal management, affecting our way of feeling and our way of thinking.

- Feelings of sadness often well up within me.

- At the end of the day, I have more negative thoughts than positive ones.

- I have hardly any interest in having sex.

- At times I have thought about taking my own life.

- Sometimes I find myself crying over unimportant issues.

- In everyday life, I feel trapped.

- I feel lonely.

- Every little task I do takes a lot of effort to complete.

Highly sensitive people can feel everything around them more intensely than the rest of the population, but they feel everything, both good and bad. They perceive and process stimuli with great intensity, therefore, they absorb positive and negative stimuli which affect their health in different ways, depending on the result of having lived some experiences or others. Positive stimuli generate positive emotions in the person, such as joy, tranquility, or happiness. Negative stimuli, on the other hand, can lead to depression in the highly sensitive person. The perception of stimuli is a very subjective thing, the same situation or the same degree of stress can cause illness or not cause illness depending on how the individual in question feels it and how they process it in their mind.

Perceiving other people's negative emotions, such as rage, anger, frustration, or phobias, can exhaust the HSP's sensitivity, even causing illnesses such as depression. Sometimes, this negativity of the other person is hidden, it is not visible to the naked eye, it simply manifests itself through unpredictable behaviors such as shouting, foul language, or indifference. Highly sensitive people need to stay away from toxic people who can plunge them into depression.

On other occasions, what can generate depression are precisely the cognitive schemes that the highly sensitive person establishes in his mind to understand the world. It is usually due to the implantation of misconceptions or cognitive distortions. For example, being subjected to constant environmental stimuli that are annoying for the HSP, such as lights, noise, waiting in line, etc. may be extenuating factors in triggering a latent disorder. Many HSP people have already learned to avoid going to large shopping malls during the holidays or sales, to avoid rush hour traffic, and to choose where to spend their leisure time, thus avoiding overstimulation that, when taken to the extreme, can lead to discouragement and even depression.

According to the Diagnostic and Statistical Manual of Mental Disorders, depression is a mood disorder characterized by the presence of many of the following factors: sadness, irritability, anhedonia or lack of satisfaction, deterioration in relationships with other people, apathy or listlessness, psychomotor slowing, alterations in memory or attention, lack of concentration, and even thoughts of death or suicide in the most severe cases. In addition, depression can manifest along with other psycho-physiological alterations, such as sleep disturbances, fatigue, loss of appetite, loss of sexual desire, and diffuse body discomfort.

According to Vallejo (2010), depression is conceptualized in terms of the degree of satisfaction and dissatisfaction of the person concerning their own activities and plans. If the balance is positive, the person feels good emotionally. If, on the other hand, dissatisfaction predominates, it can lead to reduced activity, low self-esteem, and negative emotional and physiological changes. However, it is the perception of each person that determines whether the quality of a stimulus is positive or not.

Although the word depression is used colloquially to describe someone who is sad and listless, when it is a one-time occurrence or an isolated or momentary behavior that passes as you continue your routine, it would not be a depressive disorder. According to Garcia-Vera and Sanz (2005), the factors that will indicate whether we are talking about a temporary discouragement or a depressive disorder are the frequency, duration, and intensity of the symptoms, as well as the situations in which the person manifests these symptoms. For example, a depressed person cries in sad situations in the same way that a non-depressed person does, however, what characterizes a person with depressive disorder is crying in neutral or even happy situations, thus reinforcing the maladaptive behavior that we call a symptom.

Another way to reinforce the behaviors of the person with depression will depend on the role of those close to them. When the social context maintains the belief that depression is an illness and therefore the patient must be protected, cared for, or kept at rest, it contributes to the maintenance of observable depressive symptoms, such as doing fewer things, crying, or eating less. In addition to observable symptoms, the person with depression suffers from unobservable cognitions or mental elements, which can only be manifested through verbal communication, whether oral, written, or graphic. Therefore, it is essential that if we suspect that a person who is close to us is suffering from depressive symptoms, we should encourage them to seek professional help. Psychiatrists and psychologists are the appropriate people to treat them.

Beck's Cognitive Theory, 1983, bases the cognitive model of depression on three concepts: the cognitive triad, schemas, and cognitive distortions. The cognitive triad refers to three patterns, the person's negative view of themselves, their tendency to interpret their experiences negatively, and their negative view of the future. Schemas are stable patterns in the way of interpreting situations, which can be activated at any time and which in depressive patients are shown to be inappropriate and beyond their voluntary control. Regarding cognitive distortions, depression is primitive, global, absolute, unchanging, and irreversible thinking, which refers to the person and not to the behavior.

To treat this rigidity of thinking that occurs in people with depression, many psychologists turn to Beck's cognitive therapy for depression, which is defined as an active, directive, structured, time-limited, directive procedure. The therapeutic relationship must be based on trust, rapport (psychological and emotional attunement between two people), and patient-therapist collaboration. Active participation by the patient is necessary for this to work. It is important to modify the patient's thoughts in a didactic way, but allow and encourage them to discover this for themselves. The general goals to establish are the elimination of depressive symptoms and relapse prevention.

When the person suffering from depression is highly sensitive, the psychologist must be properly informed and trained about the characteristics of the HSP trait to tune in with the patient and establish an adequate therapeutic relationship. First of all, the patient must accept having this trait if he is not yet aware of it. The psychologist must provide him with the existing information about highly sensitive people, and show him the positive side and advantages of being an HSP. In most cases, patients begin by blaming their trait as the culprit for their depression, which makes the work of treatment more arduous in the early stages. Once the patient has accepted his or her role as an HSP patient, that is, knows that a highly sensitive person is someone who is born with certain characteristics, not necessarily negative, and is also aware of his or her depressive symptoms, therapy can progress optimally.

ARIADNA 54 YEARS OLD

Ariadna had always lived with her family, the eldest of 9 siblings, she was left without a father at the age of 12 and had to assume the role of father and mother when her mother left home to work long days. When she formed her own family, she had a son and devoted herself, body and soul, to him and her partner. She always felt misunderstood and different, but she kept going, struggling to survive in a world that was increasingly stacked against her. After her divorce, she became so distant from her son that she thought it was the worst thing that had ever happened to her. She was afraid of failing as a mother, after having failed as a wife.

The way that both her son and her partner had treated her, had caused her to have continuous feelings of guilt. They would make her feel as if their suffering was all her fault. In addition, they had become compulsive controllers, criticizing every one of Ariadna's actions. Like many others like her, Ariadna had fallen victim to the common results of living with obsessive-compulsive people. People who always give their opinion, even unsolicited advice, or are always talking about what the other person should do and are determined to point out everything that the other person does wrong. These types of people make HSPs feel depressed, exhausted and trapped by their verbal attacks because they take their judgments and injustices seriously.

Ariadna became ill with cancer, and to her surprise, none of the people to whom she had dedicated her whole life came to offer help. She searched for information about depression and self-esteem and came across something she didn't know about, High Sensitivity. She found the light she needed to move forward on her own, as she understood why she felt different than most of her family members. She learned to surround herself with people who gave her peace and quiet. Today, Ariadna thinks that thanks to cancer she "took the veil from her eyes" and realized that she didn't need anything from the people who caused her so much pain and that she had to fight for herself. Always thinking of others, she had never considered that she was the most important thing in her own life. Now she lives happily and has many friends, she lives without fear of failure, although she does not forget that depression is nothing compared to the "pit" into which she had fallen.

References:

Bados, A. (2008). Beck's Cognitive Therapy. F.J. Labrador (Coor.), Cognitive Behavior Therapy (pg. 517-533). Madrid: Piramide.

Curran, J. P. (1985). Social Skills Therapy: A Model and a Treatment. R. M. Turner; L. M. Ascher (Eds.), Evaluating Behavior Therapy Outcome, 122-123. New York: Springer.

Eysenck, H. J. (1953). The Structure of Human Personality. Methuen.

Maslow, A. H. (1943). Preface to Motivation Theory. Psychosomatic Medicine, 5, 85–92. https://doi.org/10.1097/00006842-194301000-00012

Monjas, I. and Caballo, V. E. (2002). Psychopathology and Treatment of Childhood Shyness. Caballo and Simon (Eds.), Handbook of Clinical Child and Adolescent Psychology (pp. 271-296). Editorial Pirámide.

Mustaca Alba, E.. (2006). Review of "Psychological Therapy with Children and Adolescents. Clinical Case Studies". Méndez Carrillo, F. X.. Espada Sánchez, J. P. and Orgilés Amorós, M. (Coords.). Interdisciplinary, 23 (2).

Opazo, R., Andreani, M. A. and Alliende, F. (1983). Beck's Cognitive Therapy for Depression and its Relationships with Bandura's Self-Efficacy Theory.

Psychological Therapy, 2 (2), 22–55.,

Orgilés, M., Espada, J.P., García-Fernández, J.M., Méndez,F.X. and Hidalgo, M.D. (2011). Most Feared Situations Related to Separation Anxiety and Characteristics by Age and Gender in Late Childhood. Psychology Annals 27, 80-85.

Sanz, J., García Vera, M., Espinosa, R., Fortún, M. and Vázquez Valverde, C. (2005). Spanish Adaptation of Beck-II Depression Inventory (BDI-II): 3. Psychometric Properties in Patients with Psychological Disorders. Clinic and Health, 16(2), 121–142.

Vallejo, A. and Zuleta, K. (2019). Depression, Anxiety, and Physical Activity in School-aged Children: Comparative Study.

Chapter 8. Highly Sensitive Patients

HSPs seek professional help when they feel they have a wounded soul. They feel different, but they know they can solve the pain that keeps them from getting ahead in their lives. Psychologists know that addressing this need on time, prevents the patient from developing a disorder. In the same way, signs appear in children to indicate that they need help.

On the other hand, possessing the trait of high sensitivity can lead to a positive strategy in the development of the individual, depending largely on the parenting style in which the child is immersed. Parental educational styles, knowledge of the trait, and social interaction can be decisive in avoiding a disorder, or in attending to and correcting a difficulty in time.

8.1 What concerns High Sensitivity professionals

We know that labels can negatively affect a child's development. But we also know that giving a name to a certain profile can help to solve present difficulties as well as those that may arise in the future. Specialists are concerned with the best social, emotional, and intellectual development of the child. Therefore, it is the professionals who are in the best position, if the family agrees, to decide when it is necessary to go to the dreaded or desired diagnosis.

A fundamental task of professionals is precisely to protect families and children from misdiagnoses and diagnoses made by unqualified personnel. High Sensitivity professionals are concerned with making known and disseminating the existence of HSC, taking into account the more scientific nature of this trait. They try to protect patients from professional intrusion that may be related to High Sensitivity, and also help them to avoid the information deluge that exists about HSC. Another important factor that High Sensitivity professionals work on is to spread the word about the needs of HSC and to raise awareness of this trait in the educational and health community.

8.2. Why HSCs are mistaken as having other disorders

Some of the behaviors that characterize HSC can be confused with symptoms belonging to certain childhood psychological disorders. For example, an HSC may become distracted when their teacher is explaining the lesson, because they are absorbed in their creative thinking. If this distractive behavior is repeated over time and also occurs in different situations, it can be confused with the most characteristic symptom of Attention Deficit Disorder. If, in addition, this is a toddler, a stage in which children can be restless by nature, it can be thought that we are dealing with a child suffering from Attention Deficit Hyperactivity Disorder.

These children may also present behaviors that can be confused with symptoms of Autism Spectrum Disorder, such as the tantrums that HSC throw when they feel misunderstood or because of how long it takes them to react when they are uncertain about a rule or following direction. They can also become irritable, resulting in misbehavior due to overstimulation leading to mistaking their emotional discomfort for a behavioral disorder.

The HSC's need for solitary time-outs after overstimulating situations can be confused with an antisocial behavior disorder. As infants whose parents have not picked up on their extreme sensitivity, HSC may express their discomfort, for example, to tissue or other environmental stimuli. In these cases, the misconception could be regarding a possible mental disorder.

Concerning information processing, the HSC may be confused with as being a high-performance student because of their information processing advantage and sensitivity to more subtle environmental stimuli.

On the other hand, we must not confuse children with high sensitivity with children with sensory integration problems. The Sensory Integration Disorder appears as part of a broader medical picture, present in general developmental difficulties which require sessions with an occupational therapist.

8.3. When being an HSC becomes a problem.

The HSC's brain tends to process everything in great detail, they are prone to be persistent and in trying to do something perfectly, they can become frustrated if they don't succeed. Also, when something goes wrong, they become overexcited, which can leave them with feelings of failure and a desire to abandon the task at hand.

When parents and their HSC do not know the source of their skin sensitivity or their heightened sense of sight or hearing, it can be upsetting. Discomfort from fabrics, feeling overwhelmed by noise and by bright lights are typical disadvantages for the HSC as they grow up.

On the other hand, although there is no specific mood state that predominates in HSC, their life experiences may affect their emotions more decisively than in other children.

8.4. When being an HSC becomes an advantage.

A highly sensitive child has many advantages from birth. It is gratifying to see how they follow everything with their eyes, pay attention to every sound, or perceive the textures of their clothes.

When they grow up, they show that they are aware of everything, and as a result, they are less exposed to dangers and think carefully about the consequences of their actions. They also develop great empathy, which favors their social interaction. They care about when others are treated unjustly, becoming great friends of their friends.

HSC tend to be intuitive, reflective, and creative, due to their way of processing information. Qualities that, if well developed, will be factors that favor the child and his or her development as a person. Sensitivity to the subtleties of the environment can become an asset for some HSC. Thanks to this ability some grow up to become good sportsmen or great musicians.

8.5. What I can do when teaching HSC?

Teachers and educators play a critical role in the life of any child and for the HSC they can become truly significant. Both parties will hit it off if the teacher is also a highly sensitive person (HSP), or if he/she is a creative and empathetic person.

However, during their school years, children come across many teachers and educators, and the adaptation must be mutual. Hence the importance of keeping informed about how the HSC performs so that the teacher can achieve the best classroom performance. We know that teaching is an arduous task. Teachers work with diverse groups of children each with an individual temperament and peculiar upbringing. Knowing how an HSC feels and how they may act will facilitate the difficult task teachers face every day in the classroom.

According to studies carried out to date in other countries, 15% of the population is Highly Sensitive. Clinical data collected in Spain by the Spanish Association of Psychologists and Professionals of High Sensitivity (PAS Spain) show that there are approximately between 8% and 10% of HSC in Spain. Therefore, in each educational facility, we will find this percentage of HSC students. However, these data are for reference only, as the questionnaires are currently being evaluated to provide a more accurate assessment and classification.

Teachers can identify an HSC in the classroom and implement measures of care together with the counselor, if necessary. Such measures will have to be personalized, as each HSC has their own particular way of acting in relation to how their trait is expressed. In general, educators will be able to implement the following guidelines:

• Keep in mind that it will be of great help if they are creative teachers in the classroom.

• Break down tasks to prevent overload.

• Warn the students of any changes in the routine and even with the youngest ones, be sure to warn them of the transition from one activity to another.

• Do not be harsh when correcting the student, as a gentle correction will be sufficient for an HSC.

• Explain to them the consequences of being part of a group, as HSC are outraged by what they see as social injustices.

• Help them make friends. HSC are good at making friends one on one. They can thrive socially if they sit at the beginning of the school year with some like-minded or familiar children.

• Give them time to solve their social problems,

helping them before they become frustrated.

• Keep in mind that the HSC will adapt best to a quiet, low-noise, and not too hot classroom environment. If the teacher notices that the HSC is anxious, it may be due to any of these physical factors.

• Getting them used to speaking in public from an early age, always respecting their own pace, will be beneficial to them when they reach higher stages. The progression can go from small to large, starting with voluntary participation or presentations with partners.

• Making the HSC feel safe, thus preventing problems before they arise, will be easy by achieving the same level of stimulation and protection. Try to make every step successful for the HSC.

8.6. When should I seek help for my HSC?

We always feel an enormous responsibility for the needs of the little ones. The importance of HSC parenting establishes the need to avoid depression and anxiety in adulthood. Other health risks of disregarding high sensitivity are related to the lack of ability to manage one's own emotions, as well as the lack of social skills for the sake of isolation.

Both education and health play important roles in the development of HSC. When everything is going well and the child is functioning optimally, that is, no problems are arising from his or her trait, it is not necessary to seek professional help. This is different from any psychological disorder such as pervasive developmental disorders, for which early care offers improved opportunities for the infant's or toddler's physical, intellectual and social development. On the other hand, HSC require the same stimulation at an early age as any other child who does not suffer from any pathology.

Problems in HSC do not arise simply because they are born with their characteristic trait. When difficulties arise, they do so as a result of their interaction with the environment. We know that a good upbringing, caring for the needs that may arise, educational, emotional, or social, will be sufficient for the optimal evolutionary development of the HSC. If their creativity or sensitivity is also stimulated in any of the senses shown by the HSC, as they grow, they will demonstrate greater than average ability in that particular area. In other words, HSC have great potential, which, if well managed, will bear fruit.

In summary, it must be said that HSC are not born with an impairment, rather they are born with a potential that can be stimulated. Problems can arise when the upbringing is not optimal. Professional help should be sought when there are doubts during parenting and the HSC has a special need, then it will be time to go to the school counselor, pediatrician, or child psychologist.

8.7. What can I do as a parent of an HSC?

Parents of highly sensitive children can sense there is going to be a challenge even from the time they are very young. Even as early as a few days old, babies can show signs that indicate their high sensitivity.

As they get older, the signals increase. Some HSC increase their attachment to a parent or need more affection from others. Others require more playtime or more rest time.

The guidelines for parents to follow regarding parenting their HSC vary depending on the age of the child. Other factors may play a role as well, such as whether their parents also identify with the trait of high sensitivity. It is also necessary to be attentive to the emergence of psychological symptoms derived from the trait and its interaction with the environment.

Above all, we must remember that this is not a disorder to be treated, but rather a personality trait that needs to be addressed to meet latent needs. Some general guidelines for HSC parents to follow are:

• Observe the attitude that the parents themselves have towards their HSC, to change strategies that are not working.

• Talk about the problem that is causing them to have such intense feelings to be able to provide them with guidance on how to manage their emotions and feelings.

• Protect without overprotecting, observe from a distance to be attentive to their needs and the possible onset of symptoms of discomfort.

• Act naturally around children with the highly sensitive trait so as not to make them feel different or worse than others.

• Show confidence and spontaneity with the way they act, never pity.

• Be firm in the way you educate, set rules and limits, without allowing them to use their vulnerability to get their way.

• Have a lot of patience, sometimes it is better to take a longer road to achieve the goal.

• Train your child not to develop feelings of guilt about everything that happens.

• Prevent them from taking on responsibilities that do not pertain to their role.

• Allow your child to express emotions, even negative ones such as sadness, fear, or anger.

• Be alert in case any symptom appears as a result of an emotional psychological problem.

In the face of an unfavorable upbringing for the HSC, low self-esteem could be an issue for the child. All parental actions should be oriented towards the improvement and optimal development of the HSC's self-perception. It is also important not to forget that each HSC is unique. Studies show different levels of sensitivity among people, as well as differences between the education received and one's own school, social, and family experiences.

The sooner you detect that a child is HSC, the sooner you can begin to improve their surroundings. It is essential to avoid the emergence of emotional distress arising from the trait. It is just as important to promote a healthy environment where good self-esteem is fostered and anxiety is avoided.

8.8. What do statistics say about HSC, regarding culture, gender, and genetics.

Studies of HSC families confirm the hypothesis of possible genetic transmission from parents to children. Therefore, it is an inherited trait although there is still a lot of research work to be done in this regard.

In terms of gender, there are no significant differences in the percentages of children with the trait of high sensitivity. There is no relationship between being a girl or a boy HSC, except in the way emotions are externalized, just as they can occur in a child who is not highly sensitive.

In conclusion, it could be said that due to their characteristics, HSC may feel more secure and comfortable immersed in Eastern culture than in Western culture. Traditionally, Eastern culture bases happiness on the understanding of the inner world, as opposed to the Western concept that bases happiness on appearances, ego, and consumerism. Likewise, the expression of feelings is in plain sight in the oriental culture, which avoids altering the nature of things. Faced with difficulties, Eastern culture prefers to avoid them rather than solve them, since they consider that problems upset their balance.

The diverse lifestyles according to the culture, make

HSC from Eastern countries feel very fulfilled and become great leaders. In our culture, we can also be proud to see how sensitivity is changing and is no longer seen as a defect or as something that is only feminine. Every day there are signs of how sensitivity is being lived and perceived as a strength of enormous usefulness, both for personal, social relations, as well as for the workplace. If we trust that this change is incremental, we may see the HSC of today become successful HSPs in the future.

References:

Aron, E. N. and A. Aron. (1997). Sensory-processing Sensitivity and its Relation to Introversion and Emotionality. J. Pers. Soc. Psychol. 73: 345– 368.

Gerstenberg, F.X.R. (2012). Sensory-processing Sensitivity Predicts Performance on a Visual Search Task Followed by an Increase in Perceived Stress, Personality and Individual Differences, Volume 53, Issue 4, 2012, Pages 496-500. https://doi.org/10.1016/j.paid.2012.04.019.

Gross, J. J., and John, O.P. (2003). Individual Differences in Two Emotion Regulation Processes: Implications for Affect, Relationships, and Well-being. J. Pers. Soc. Psychol. 85: 348– 32.

Hofmann, S. G. and Bitran, S. (2007). Sensory-processing Sensitivity in Social Anxiety Disorder: Relationship to Harm Avoidance and Diagnostic Subtypes. J. Anxiety Disord. 21: 944– 954.

Jagiellowicz, J., Aron, A. and Aron, E.N. (2016). Relation Between the Temperament Trait of Sensory Processing Sensitivity and Emotional Reactivity. Soc. Behav. Pers., 44 (2) (2016), pp. 185-200

Jagiellowicz, J., Zarinafsar, S. and Acevedo, B.P. (2020). Health and Social Outcomes in Highly Sensitive Persons.

Meyer, B., M. Ajchenbrenner and Bowles, D.P. (2005). Sensory Sensitivity, Attachment Experiences, and Rejection Responses Among Adults with Borderline and Avoidant Features. J. Pers. Disord. 19: 641– 658.

Pluess, M. and Belsky, J. (2013). Vantage Sensitivity: Individual Differences in Response to Positive Experiences. Psychol. Bull. 139: 901– 916.

Suomi, S.J. (1997). Early Determinants of Behavior: Evidence from Primate Studies. British Medical Bulletin, 53(1),170–184.

Wolf, M., Van Doorn, S. and Weissing, F.J. (2008). Evolutionary Emergence of Responsive and Unresponsive Personalities. PNAS 105: 15825– 15830.

Chapter 9. Problems derived from high sensitivity.

9.1. How to act in social situations if you are an HSP

As we have explained in other chapters, many highly sensitive people do not present problems that should be treated in consultation with psychologists or psychiatrists since they adapt perfectly to their environment and can go fairly unnoticed. They can easily carry on with life naturally despite the neurodiversity related to their trait. When an HSP adapts well to their environment, they don't need to go to a mental health specialist, at least, not just because they are an HSP. However, many of them find their trait becoming a great handicap when it comes to living with their partner or their children, or simply before any social interaction. However, the HSP is not the source of the difficulty, but rather, the problem is the others. In these cases, the solution is to search for information about the personality types that exist and learn to use the appropriate role.

According to the psychology and psychiatry manuals, there are three main personality disorder groups (Groups: A, B, and C). We will define them and then explain how to act around them if you are an HSP.

GROUP A

Paranoid personality disorder: Are people who

distrust others, doubt everyone else's loyalty, are reluctant to trust people, or they are convinced that any information they give can be used against them. They see hidden threats, hold grudges, feel like they or their reputation is being attacked, and unjustly suspect their partner of being unfaithful. Children with PPD go through a phase of fear of strangers.

Schizoid personality disorder: They neither desire nor enjoy personal relationships, or even being part of a family. They always choose solitary activities, have no interest in having sexual experiences with another person and they do not enjoy almost any activity. They do not have intimate friends or people they trust, except for first-degree relatives, as in parents or children. They are indifferent to the flattery or criticism of others and can have a limited range of emotional expression appearing emotionally cold, distant, or unaffectionate.

Schizotypal personality disorder: They present a general pattern of acute discomfort in social settings. They lack social and interpersonal skills and a reduced capacity for personal relationships, as well as perceptual distortions and eccentric behavior.

They are also likely to have odd beliefs, be suspicious, superstitious, feel they are clairvoyant, have delusional body illusions or strange perceptual experiences such as thinking they have special powers, as well as bizarre fantasies and language, inappropriate or restricted affectivity, odd or eccentric appearance and behavior, lack of close friends and distrust of first-degree relatives. They suffer from social anxiety that does not diminish with familiarization which is associated with paranoid fears and not with negative judgments about themselves.

Relationships between an HSP and a person with a Group A Disorder: The highly sensitive person should be protected from those individuals with covert hostility since their smiling facade is hiding rage. In addition, they may seem sincere at first, but they are not trustworthy. They promise, but they do not fulfill their promises. Living or having a close relationship with this type of person can generate depression in the highly sensitive person, since they conceal their continuous anger and their feeling of rage or frustrations, which easily causes the HSP to start having feelings of guilt. For example, people in Group A could utter sarcastic remarks only to quickly dismiss them as "just a joke", or forget their partner's anniversary knowing full well how important it is to them. To live with this type of individual, highly sensitive people must acquire good communication skills and encourage the growth of their own self-esteem.

GROUP B: Excessively extroverted, emotional, impulsive, unstable, and immature individuals.

Antisocial personality disorder: They show a general pattern of contempt and violation of the rights of others exhibiting failure to adapt to social norms, dishonesty, impulsivity, irritability, or aggressiveness. They are usually reckless about their safety or that of others and persistently behave irresponsibly, without feelings of remorse.

Borderline personality disorder: They experience a general pattern of unstable intense relationships alternating between periods of idealizing somebody and then devaluing them. They experience changes in self-identity, self-image, or sense of self. Unable to establish stable relationships due to their mood swings, with episodes of dysphoria, irritability, and anxiety, impulsivity which is manifested in behaviors such as spending sprees, substance abuse, or reckless driving. They have an intense fear of abandonment, going to extreme measures to avoid real or imagined separation or rejection; recurrent suicide attempts or threats and self-harming behavior; chronic feelings of emptiness, inappropriate and intense anger, and uncontrolled bad temper. Sometimes they also experience paranoid ideation or dissociative symptoms.

Histrionic personality disorder: These are people with exaggerated emotional reactions who are constantly seeking attention from others. They are usually uncomfortable in situations in which they are not the center of attention. Their interaction with others can be characterized by inappropriate sexually seductive or provocative behavior. Their emotional expression is shallow and shifts quickly. Their way of speaking is excessively subjective with exaggerated expression of emotion, self-dramatization, and theatricality. In addition, they are easily influenced by others. They usually consider a relationship more intimate than it is in reality.

Narcissistic personality disorder: They are people who crave attention and lack any empathy. They have an inflated sense of self-importance, exaggerate their achievements, and expect to be recognized as superior. Their fantasies of success are unlimited. They believe they are special or unique and that only people who are special or have a higher status can understand them. They expect excessive admiration and become unhappy when their unreasonable expectations of receiving special favor or treatment are not met. A person with a narcissistic personality disorder is exploitative in their relationships and tries to take advantage of others.

They do not recognize the feelings and needs of others, are usually envious, and think that they are envied in turn. They generally display arrogance and haughtiness.

Relationships between an HSP and a person with a Group B Disorder: Highly sensitive people must be cautious when dealing with someone they know falls into the category of this disorder since they may seem to be positive at first, but these always turn into toxic relationships. The HSP will give of themselves freely and completely because of their big-heartedness and empathy but will end up being manipulated and unfulfilled. A person suffering from these disorders is generally someone who attacks by discrediting, criticizing and guilt-tripping, and thoroughly enjoys humiliating and ostracizing their partner. Faced with this type of individual, the highly sensitive person must act courageously, anticipating the outcomes of situations and planning strategies of action. It is important to ignore their intentional criticisms and seek professional help if the person suffering from any of these disorders has damaged the self-esteem of the person who is highly sensitive, or if the situation has gone to the point of generating anxiety or depression. This is likely because the HSPs feel more intensely, therefore, they are more susceptible to situations that generate extreme emotions.

GROUP C

Avoidant Personality Disorder: The people who suffer from it present a general pattern of extreme social inhibition, feelings of inferiority, and hypersensitivity to negative reactions. They usually avoid jobs and activities that involve interpersonal contact for fear of criticism or rejection. They are often reluctant to get into a relationship and are repressive in intimate relationships for fear of ridicule.

Dependent personality disorder: Affects people with an excessive need to be taken care of causing in them a behavior of submission, clinginess, and separation anxiety. They have difficulty making everyday decisions unless they have an excessive amount of advice from others. They need others to assume responsibility for major life decisions. They have a hard time disagreeing with people because of fear of losing support, also difficulty starting projects due to a lack of confidence in their own judgment. They are even willing to tolerate doing unpleasant tasks just to maintain or gain what they perceive as protection and support from others.

Obsessive-compulsive personality disorder: These are people who excessively care about order, details, standards, organization, schedules, to the point of losing sight of the main objective of the activity. This causes them to be unable to finish almost anything they set out to do because of their self-imposed, strict demands. Their excessive dedication to work and productivity comes at the expense of missing out on leisure and engaging in activities with friends. They show excessive stubbornness, scrupulousness, and inflexibility in moral issues. Sometimes they are unable to throw useless objects, even if they do not even have a sentimental value, which is commonly known as hoarding. They are reluctant to delegate tasks and are often very frugal since they believe that it is necessary to save in case there is a future catastrophe.

Relationships between an HSP and a person with a GROUP C Disorder: Highly sensitive people must be protected from critical individuals and compulsive controllers, those who constantly offer unsolicited advice and point out the mistakes and failures of others. Taking into account that HSPs are very responsible by nature, they will easily take all the criticism and admonition to heart leading them into a possible state of depression over time. It is important to know that listening to different opinions does not mean having to heed all the advice that is received, each person is free to make their own decisions. Training in assertiveness and communication skills can help HSPs who have to live with people from

Group C.

Likewise, highly sensitive people are very creative and active and can be affected by relationships in which isolation, sadness, and apathy are prevalent. This environment will cause them anxiety and low self-esteem. HSPs are motivated, follow through with their projects, and are able to look for the positive side of everything if they live good experiences. On the other hand, they can be affected adversely by the negative experience of living with people or an inactive partner. It can be said that there are two things that "kill slowly", cancer and indifference.

9.2. Mindfulness to help highly sensitive people

The psychological technique called Mindfulness or full attention consists of training the person to focus on the present moment actively and reflexively. The goal is to learn to be fully resent and aware of the moment. It is difficult for the HSP to focus their attention on the here and now in their day-to-day life, as well as knowing how to face reality or avoid daydreaming. Mindfulness is about observing without judging, accepting each experience as it is or as it is happening, it is an evaluation of reality devoid of criticism.

Highly sensitive people may go to a consultation to deal with the effects of sensory overload which in turn interferes with their depth of processing. They reflect deeply about themselves, their past, their family, or their choice of friends as well as worry about death or suffering. A mind that is constantly revisiting the past and coming back to the present will need to seek professional help from psychologists or psychotherapists.

Being able to exist in the world without prejudices, open to sensory experience, in tune with it, and not actively rejecting it, is a phenomenon of interest for highly sensitive people. The task of the psychologist, in this case, is to establish how the HSP can focus their attention and adjust their actions to adapt to each situation in positive terms and by pointing out the issues that arise from not focusing on the here and now, according to the training.

The Mindfulness training technique includes teaching the individual to observe their body and their thoughts and describe them while trying to suspend judgment but focusing on the moment. It is a type of Zen meditation based on the eastern culture ideal of living in the present moment mixed with psychological contributions from the personality construct, acceptance and commitment therapy, or other conducive therapies.

The method of application of the technique consists largely in progressive relaxation, the observation of the behavior without trying to control it, acceptance of any sensation that occurs without struggling or trying to control the movement or change that the behavior produces. The actual exercises can be very diverse and include breath training, relaxation techniques, and self-guidance. For a more detailed exercise study, we recommend looking into the autogenic training technique developed by Johannes Schultz; Mindfulness-Based Stress Reduction Program by Kabat-Zinn; Dialectical Behavior Therapy by Marsha; Mindfulness-Based Cognitive Therapy by Segal; Or the acceptance and commitment therapy developed by Hayes.

Negative emotions, such as shame, anger, sadness,

fear, or anxiety, can be normal, generally speaking, for the average person. However, we know that a highly sensitive person tends to experience very intense and frequent emotions, including those that are negative. Therefore, HSPs can benefit from training in Mindfulness to adopt a personality not based on rejecting or suppressing thoughts, but quite the opposite, accepting them as they are. It is not about facing the feelings of tension, anger, or anguish, rather, it is about learning to live with them, because "what you are feeling is part of you."

Vallejo (2010) speaks of Mindfulness, a phenomenon of obvious interest in psychology, as a way to get involved in the usual activities, whether they are problematic or not. The technique consists of feeling things as they happen, without looking for ways to control them. It is not about focusing on a thought to exchange it with a positive one, as in other psychological techniques. It is about accepting the experiences and sensations as they happen at that specific moment, thus allowing the presence of each experience without replacing it with what needs to happen or happened in past similar situations. Likewise, it has to do with putting stimuli and emotions ahead of their interpretation. Thought and language have an immense power to cover up what is seen and felt, even if it is obvious. Very often, words replace reality, conforming the experience to rigid thought structures or stereotypes. Prejudices contribute to misrepresenting experiences thus missing out on the wealth of feeling produced by the variability of perceptions and emotions.

Psychologists tell us that it also consists in the non-judgemental acceptance of the experience, accepting the experience as it is, both the positive and the negative, and both the perfect and the imperfect. Putting up with experiences as natural and normal, although it is obvious that something more positive and pleasant may be preferable. The technique asks us to accept an unpleasant experience equally, since it is also ours, whether we like it better or we like it less. By accepting the situation in question without generating a value judgment on it, it allows us not to reject it or flee from it.

When applying the technique there should always be a direct intention to focus on something, the person chooses what to look at, act on, or think about. Although it seems that Mindfulness encourages the individual to allow themselves to be carried off, it is not like that, each person selects their goals, projects, and values in life. However, once the individual is immersed in the situation chosen, directly or indirectly, he must live it as it is, accepting everything that comes with it. In addition, the subject should not seek to control the reactions, feelings, or emotions, but to let them flow as they arise, even if they are negative, such as fear, anger, sadness, or anguish.

This is the way to make the Mindfulness technique effective in psychological therapy, although this seems somewhat contradictory to most psychological techniques which are aimed at reducing activation, controlling anxiety, or eliminating negative thoughts.

9.3. Troubleshooting as therapy for highly sensitive people

Troubleshooting therapy is used to improve social competence and to reduce psychological discomfort due to specific problems that an individual has to deal with throughout his or her life. Specifically, highly sensitive people benefit from this therapy because it has the advantage of being useful to address any type of problem. These can be interpersonal problems, such as an acquired struggle linked to fear of social judgment derived from bad experiences, or difficulty in making decisions, or displaying a more individualistic cultural trend. It can also solve intrapersonal problems, such as depression, anxiety, or post-traumatic stress.

A reason that often leads a highly sensitive patient to seek a psychologist's consultation is that they are more affected by a traumatic experience and more easily overwhelmed than other types of patients. Situations experienced with great excitement can lead them to dissociate themselves to a certain degree from reality, that is, to distance themselves from the experiences at a physical and emotional level. Troubleshooting therapy has the advantage of being carried out in the person's natural environment or real world so they can find positive consequences and avoid or decrease the negative.

Emotions which are determinants for a highly sensitive person also have an important role in troubleshooting. For there to be emotional activation when solving problems, we must guide the solution concerning three aspects: the objectivity of the problematic situation, how the individual guides his problem, and their unique problem-solving style.

An emotional response, if positive, can facilitate the problem-solving process. If negative, it can interfere with this process. Objective problematic situations are usually aversive, generating negative emotional responses in the patient, such as frustration, ambiguity, pain, or loss of reinforcers. A patient can respond to a problem in one of two ways. If the person is easily frustrated, something that happens easily to the highly sensitive person, he or she may see the problem as something overwhelming and impossible to solve. On the contrary, they can view it as something normal in their life and deal with it accordingly. And, finally, the problem-solving style can be adaptive, allowing them to solve it. Or on the contrary, it can be a style based on avoidance or impulsivity, complicating the solution process.

Positive emotional responses help optimal problem-solving. If during the process we find negative emotions that hinder problem-solving therapy, we must treat them with cognitive techniques, such as relaxation, systematic desensitization, or training in stress inoculation. When the patient has learned to control these emotions, we could apply troubleshooting therapy.

Becoña (2010) considers problem-solving therapy an effective clinical intervention. The application of therapy after establishing an adequate therapeutic relationship and once the individual capacity of the patient and their orientation towards the problem has been evaluated includes the following steps: definition of the problem, generation of alternative solutions, decision-making, implementation of the decisions taken, and checking the solution.

Among the advantages of being highly sensitive, we have highlighted that most are thoughtful, intuitive, creative, and intelligent people, due to the quality of deep processing of the present information which are virtues innate to them. These virtues favor the success of troubleshooting therapy since the initial phase of guidance towards the problem would be fundamental but feasible and includes: encouraging the belief of self-efficacy, recognizing the problem, attitude of challenge towards the problem, using emotions, as well as stopping and thinking before acting. Assuming that the problem has a solution, the next phase is also of utmost importance. That phase is defining the problem. This process includes collecting information about the factors that generated the problem in the first place, clarifying why this situation is a problem, and setting a realistic goal. This goal must be based on distinguishing whether the problem is simple or complex, if it is divisible in subproblems, or even if this problem has a solution, which can be labeled a rigid situation. Each rigid situation must be tackled as a problem to which the only solution is to accept it exists since it has no solution. Examples of this type of problem are the loss of a family member or being diagnosed with a chronic disease.

Regarding the rest of the steps to be followed in troubleshooting, practical techniques such as brainstorming to seek alternatives, postponement of judgment so as not to immediately evaluate each alternative, imaginative role-playing to anticipate the results of the decision, comparing possible outcomes, preparing a plan, self-observation of the chosen behavior, self-assessment, and self-correction to strengthen execution and perceived control.

9.4 Systemic family therapy applied to families with HSP members

Systemic family therapy consists of an integrating approach to treatment based on the relationship between the patient and the family or other significant people in the person's life. This is a group therapy that addresses communication and other social skills contextually in terms of the interaction of the individual with other family members, trying to solve adaptive problems, both their own and those attached to other struggles. The interaction between the transformation, the feedback, and the communication, are the key elements in this therapy.

Rodríguez-Arias and Venero (2006), consider the answer to the question as to why the problem persists as an essential element of Brief Strategic Family Therapy treatment. They aim to establish what prevents patients from resolving their family problems, despite their will to solve them. According to the authors, complaints are due to ineffective solution attempts.

Highly sensitive people can spend years attempting fruitless solutions, especially when there are no other members of their family with the trait, or if they feel misunderstood. They experience trouble trying to adapt their trait to the world around them, distorting intrapersonal and interpersonal functions. That is, the perception of intimacy, closeness or distance to others, support received, or feelings of loneliness, which are inherent in HSPs with an adaptive disorder, are influenced by factors related to how the individual relates to significant people in their life.

The behavior associated with the role played by a person as a member of the family, or as a member of a close family group, a friend, or workmate, is determined by certain rules linked to the system or context in question. The goal of systemic therapy is to change the patterns of interaction between group members to achieve a more adaptive behavior. It implies the identification of behaviors that need to change, positive reinforcement, and assessment of what has been achieved.

Family members, during the first sessions, focus on blaming others or themselves as a defense mechanism or justification strategy. HSPs tend to accumulate feelings of guilt, therefore, absorbing guilt from the people they love can become quite negative for them. It is also not beneficial for them to hear that their loved ones feel guilty about something that concerns them as a member of the family. It is essential to adjust Brief Strategic Family Therapy to the particular needs of the HSP trait, performing initial individual interviews to detect if any of the members have a trait of high sensitivity. The rules that need to be followed in therapy should be explained, like the importance of not devoting the first sessions to blame-shifting among the participants. This will facilitate the success of the intervention.

The problems and concerns that cause discomfort, inconvenience, or uneasiness to people who come for a consultation can be divided into complaints and demands. Complaints are those statements made by the patient to describe the obstacle that prevents them from feeling well but that do not necessarily imply a request for intervention. In contrast, demand is when a patient requests some type of resolution or psychotherapeutic intervention. For example, a highly sensitive mother, knowledgeable and aware of her fear to speak in public and who hated going up to the blackboard since she was in school goes in for a consultation about her daughter's poor performance in school. The mother talks about currently experiencing this problem at work, since she is a teacher of adults in prison, and how her fear interferes with her daily work. Because of the recent discovery that mother and daughter are highly sensitive, she presents her complaint, asking for help for her daughter, demanding solutions to the difficulties her daughter is experiencing in school because she thinks that the same thing could happen to her.

Once the complaints and demands have been established, the therapist investigates the explanation that each person who is in therapy gives about themselves about the onset and persistence of each complaint. Changing the ideas or beliefs that people have about why the underlying reason for the complaint remains will help in resolving the problem. For example, knowing that your HSC needs order to grow up with a sense of tranquility and feel good about himself, will help the family favor the establishment of routines and reward the necessary habits. Regarding the therapeutic objectives, they are agreed upon between the members of the family in attendance and the therapist. Once the complaints have been recorded and the source of the persistent discomfort is identified, the solutions attempted so far that have been ineffective are evaluated and what changes need to be made before treatment are established. Next, the therapist will begin the questions and will begin assigning the main therapeutic comments based on the answers. And, finally, the result of the intervention will compare the initial evaluation with the outcome.

OMAR AND TADEO 4 YEARS OLD

Two four-year twin brothers, so different in their behavior as night and day. Their parents decided that Omar would go see a psychologist because he had numerous tantrums, he did not talk much, and they thought he was not interacting enough with other children. They had Tadeo as a direct comparison reference. Tadeo was quick, bold, spoke with decisiveness and clarity, besides being very popular among his school friends. In the consultation, no prior pathology was detected in Omar so he was diagnosed with maturation delay. The goal was to stimulate his speech and foster his relationships with his peers. Months of observation revealed what at first seemed obvious. Each brother had his own pace of evolutionary development. Each one had his own temperament, tastes, and interests. At the beginning of the sessions, a test was carried out to detect if either of the twins had the trait of high sensitivity. The object was to carry out a comparative study between them since this was of great concern to the family. As expected, Omar showed more items of elements of possessing the HSC items in favor of the HSC trait than his brother.

It took months of observation working both with the child as well as with the rest of the family. It was established that what at first seemed to be symptoms of maturation delay was, in fact, an authentic indicator that the child was highly sensitive. The qualities that he already possessed were the qualities hiding under the surface. Omar stood out because of his discretion since he always thought before he spoke. They had just not ever given him the chance to express himself since his mother impulsively always spoke for him. When we worked with the family to allow him to have sufficient time to express himself and respond on his own accord, everything changed. Another advantage was how selective he was when choosing his friends. He was clear on which children he felt comfortable with and which children he did not want to play or be with because he was quieter than most of the children in his class and did not like unruliness. The parents understood that they should accept the fact that their young children were different and once they did, everything would work out wonderfully.

Children are the most vulnerable members of society. They have all the attention of their parents in terms of physical, educational, and social needs. However, sometimes parents or teachers are not aware of the emotional needs of the children. The way the world is felt and perceived can vary a lot from parents to children. There is not always a mental health problem when a child does not act as he or she is expected to. It may simply be a matter of empathizing with the way they see their world and looking for the appropriate resources to meet their needs.

References

Becoña, E. and Gutiérrez-Moyano, M.M. (1987). Problem Solving Therapies: Revised. Spanish Journal of Behavioral Therapy, 5, 89-118. Rodríguez-Arias, J. L., and Venero, M. (2006). Brief Family Therapy. Guide to Systematic Psychotherapy. Madrid, Spain: CCS.

D'Zurilla, T.J. (1993). Conflict Resolving Therapy: Terapia de resolución de conflictos: Social Problem Solving, a New Approach to Clinical Intervention. Bilbao. Desclée de Brouwer.

Nezu, A.M. and Nezu, C.M. (1991). Problem Solving Training. V.E. Caballo (ed.). Handbook of Behavior Modifications and Therapy Techniques. (Pgs 527-553). Madrid. Promolibro.

Díaz-García, M. I. and Díaz-Sibaja, M. A. (2005). Daily problems of Child Behavior. M.I. Comeche and M.A. Vallejo (Coor.), Handbook of Child Behavior Therapy. Madrid: Dykinson. Schultz's Autogenic Training Technique.

Hayes, S.C., Strosahl, K.D. and Wilson, K.G. (2014). Acceptance and Commitment Therapy: The Process and Practice of Mindful Change (Mindfulness). Desclée de Brouwer.

Kabat-Zinn, J. (2003). Mindfulness-based stress reduction (MBSR). Constructivism in the Human Sciences, 8 (2),

73-83. Retrieved from https://www.proquest.com/scholarly-journals/mindfulness-based-stress-reduction-mbsr/docview/204582884/se-2?accountid=14744 Linehan's Dialectical Behavior Therapy.

Segal, Z. V., Teasdale, J. D. and Williams, J. M. G. (2004). Mindfulness-Based Cognitive Therapy: Theoretical Rationale and Empirical Status. S. C. Hayes, V. M. Follette and M. M. Linehan (Eds.), Mindfulness and acceptance: Expanding the Cognitive-Behavioral Tradition (p. 45–65). Guilford Press.

Sohst, K. (2017). The Power of Sensitivity. How to Identify Highly Sensitive People and What We Can Learn from Them. Editorial Ariel.

Vallejo, M. A. and Ruiz, M. A. (eds.) (1993). A Practical Guide for Behavior Modificaction. Madrid: Fundación Universidad Empresa.

Wilson, K. G. and Soriano, M. C. L. (2002). Acceptance and Commitment Therapy (ACT): A Values-Oriented Behavioral Treatment. Ediciones Pirámide.

9 788883 543295 1